INTERNET
Simplified®

Visual

by Paul McFedries

WILEY

Wiley Publishing, Inc.

INTERNET SIMPLIFIED®

Published by
Wiley Publishing, Inc.
10475 Crosspoint Boulevard
Indianapolis, IN 46256

www.wiley.com

Published simultaneously in Canada

Copyright © 2009 by Wiley Publishing, Inc., Indianapolis, Indiana

Library of Congress Control Number: 2008943500

ISBN: 978-0-470-40446-1

Manufactured in the United States of America

10 9 8 7 6 5 4 3 2 1

Trademark Acknowledgments

Contact Us

For general information on our other products and services please contact our Customer Care Department within the U.S. at 877-762-2974, outside the U.S. at 317-572-3993, or fax 317-572-4002.

For technical support please visit www.wiley.com/techsupport.

Wiley Publishing, Inc.

Sales
Contact Wiley at (800) 762-2974 or fax (317) 572-4002.

Praise for Visual Books

"Like a lot of other people, I understand things best when I see them visually. Your books really make learning easy and life more fun."

John T. Frey (Cadillac, MI)

"I have quite a few of your Visual books and have been very pleased with all of them. I love the way the lessons are presented!"

Mary Jane Newman (Yorba Linda, CA)

"I just purchased my third Visual book (my first two are dog-eared now!), and, once again, your product has surpassed my expectations."

Tracey Moore (Memphis, TN)

"I am an avid fan of your Visual books. If I need to learn anything, I just buy one of your books and learn the topic in no time. Wonders! I have even trained my friends to give me Visual books as gifts."

Illona Bergstrom (Aventura, FL)

"Thank you for making it so clear. I appreciate it. I will buy many more Visual books."

J.P. Sangdong (North York, Ontario, Canada)

"I have several books from the Visual series and have always found them to be valuable resources."

Stephen P. Miller (Ballston Spa, NY)

"Thank you for the wonderful books you produce. It wasn't until I was an adult that I discovered how I learn — visually. Nothing compares to Visual books. I love the simple layout. I can just grab a book and use it at my computer, lesson by lesson. And I understand the material! You really know the way I think and learn. Thanks so much!"

Stacey Han (Avondale, AZ)

"I absolutely admire your company's work. Your books are terrific. The format is perfect, especially for visual learners like me. Keep them coming!"

Frederick A. Taylor, Jr. (New Port Richey, FL)

"I have several of your Visual books and they are the best I have ever used."

Stanley Clark (Crawfordville, FL)

"I bought my first Visual book last month. Wow. Now I want to learn everything in this easy format!"

Tom Vial (New York, NY)

"Thank you, thank you, thank you...for making it so easy for me to break into this high-tech world. I now own four of your books. I recommend them to anyone who is a beginner like myself."

Gay O'Donnell (Calgary, Alberta, Canada)

"I write to extend my thanks and appreciation for your books. They are clear, easy to follow, and straight to the point. Keep up the good work! I bought several of your books and they are just right! No regrets! I will always buy your books because they are the best."

Seward Kollie (Dakar, Senegal)

"Compliments to the chef!! Your books are extraordinary! Or, simply put, extra-ordinary, meaning way above the rest! THANK YOU THANK YOU THANK YOU! I buy them for friends, family, and colleagues."

Christine J. Manfrin (Castle Rock, CO)

"What fantastic teaching books you have produced! Congratulations to you and your staff. You deserve the Nobel Prize in Education in the Software category. Thanks for helping me understand computers."

Bruno Tonon (Melbourne, Australia)

"Over time, I have bought a number of your 'Read Less - Learn More' books. For me, they are THE way to learn anything easily. I learn easiest using your method of teaching."

José A. Mazón (Cuba, NY)

"I am an avid purchaser and reader of the Visual series, and they are the greatest computer books I've seen. The Visual books are perfect for people like myself who enjoy the computer, but want to know how to use it more efficiently. Your books have definitely given me a greater understanding of my computer, and have taught me to use it more effectively. Thank you very much for the hard work, effort, and dedication that you put into this series."

Alex Diaz (Las Vegas, NV)

Credits

About the Author

Paul McFedries is a full-time technical writer. Paul has been authoring computer books since 1991 and he has more than 60 books to his credit. Paul's books have sold more than three million copies worldwide. These books include the Wiley titles *Teach Yourself VISUALLY Windows Vista*, *Windows Vista: Top 100 Simplified Tips & Tricks*, *Teach Yourself VISUALLY Computers, 5th Edition*, *Macs Portable Genius*, *iPhone 3G Portable Genius*, and *The Unofficial Guide to Microsoft Office 2007*. Paul is also the proprietor of Word Spy (www.wordspy.com), a Web site that tracks new words and phrases as they enter the language.

Author's Acknowledgments

It goes without saying that writers focus on text, and I certainly enjoyed focusing on the text that you'll read in this book. However, this book is more than just the usual collection of words and phrases. A quick thumb through the pages will show you that this book is also chock full of images, from sharp screen shots to fun and informative illustrations. Those colorful images sure make for a beautiful book, and that beauty comes from a lot of hard work by Wiley's immensely talented group of designers and layout artists. They are all listed in the Credits section on the previous page, and I thank them for creating another gem. Of course, what you read in this book must also be accurate, logically presented, and free of errors. Ensuring all of this was an excellent group of editors that included project editor Sarah Hellert, copy editor Scott Tullis, and technical editor Vince Averello. Thanks to all of you for your exceptional competence and hard work. Thanks, as well, to acquisitions editor Jody Lefevere for asking me to write this book.

Table of Contents

Learning Internet Basics

Getting on the Internet

3

Browsing the World Wide Web

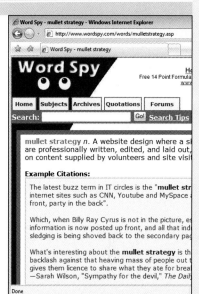

4

Surfing the Web Safely and Securely

Table of Contents

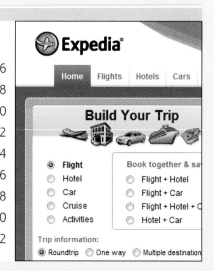

7

Working with Internet Media

8

Social Networking

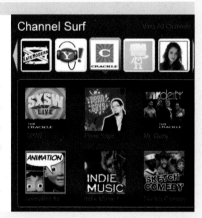

9

Buying and Selling Online

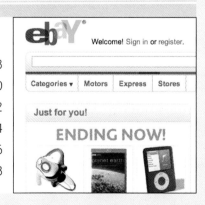

Table of Contents

10

Communicating via E-mail

11

Enhancing E-mail Security and Privacy

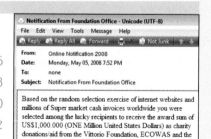

12

Communicating via Instant Messaging and Chat

13

Creating and Reading Blogs

How to Use This Book

Do you look at the pictures in a book before anything else on a page? Would you rather see an image instead of read about how to do something? Search no further. This book is for you. Opening *Internet Simplified* allows you to read less and learn more the Internet.

Who Needs This Book

This book is for a reader who has limited experience with the Internet and wants to learn more. It is also for readers who want to expand or refresh their knowledge of the different aspects of the Internet.

Book Organization

Internet Simplified has 13 chapters.

Chapter 1, **Learning Internet Basics**, gives you a brief overview of the Internet and the services it offers.

In Chapter 2, **Getting on the Internet**, you learn how to choose an Internet service provider and how to connect to the Internet.

Chapter 3, **Browsing the World Wide Web**, gives you the basics of Web browsing and shows you how to perform useful tasks such as filling in forms and saving your favorite sites.

In Chapter 4, **Surfing the Web Safely and Securely**, you learn how to protect yourself and your family while on the Internet, and you learn how to guard against specific threats such as viruses and spyware.

Chapter 5, **Searching for Information on the Web**, gives you a detailed look at how to search for the information you need using Google and other search services.

Chapter 6, **Getting Things Done on the Web**, puts the Web to work by showing you how to read news, research topics, bank and invest, find a job, and much more.

In Chapter 7, **Working with Internet Media**, you learn how to use the Internet to get music, subscribe to podcasts, listen to the radio, share photos, and watch YouTube videos.

Chapter 8, **Social Networking**, examines the social side of the Internet and shows you the basics of sites such as Facebook, MySpace, and LinkedIn.

In Chapter 9, **Buying and Selling Online**, you learn all about online shopping — including how to do comparison shopping on the Web and how to shop securely — as well as how to sell goods and services online.

Chapter 10, **Communicating via E-mail**, gives you a complete tour of the Internet's e-mail system, including how to send messages, receive messages, handle file attachments, and subscribe to mailing lists.

In Chapter 11, **Enhancing E-mail Security and Privacy**, you continue your look at e-mail with several tasks related to e-mail security and privacy.

Chapter 12, **Communicating via Instant Messaging and Chat**, shows you how to use the Internet to carry on instant messaging conversations, including text, audio, and video chats.

In Chapter 13, **Creating and Reading Blogs**, you learn all about the blogging world, including how to use sites such as TypePad and Blogger to set up your own blog.

Chapter Organization

This book consists of sections, all listed in the book's table of contents. A *section* is a set of steps that show you how to complete a specific technique. Each section, usually contained on two facing pages, has an introduction, a set of full-color screen shots and steps that walk you through the task, and a tip. This format allows you to quickly look at a topic of interest and learn it instantly.

What You Need to Use This Book

- A computer running Windows Vista or XP, or a Mac running OS X.

- For a dialup Internet connection, you need either an internal or external dialup modem connected to your computer.

- For a high-speed Internet connection, you need a broadband modem (usually provided by your Internet service provider).

- To share an Internet connection, you need a network router.

Using the Mouse

This book uses the following conventions to describe the actions you perform when using the mouse:

Click

Press your left mouse button once. You generally click your mouse on something to select something on the screen.

Double-click

Press your left mouse button twice. Double-clicking something on the computer screen generally opens whatever item you have double-clicked.

Right-click

Press your right mouse button. When you right-click anything on the computer screen, the program displays a shortcut menu containing commands specific to the selected item.

Click and Drag, and Release the Mouse

Move your mouse pointer and position it over an item on the screen. Press and hold down the left mouse button. Now, move the mouse to where you want to place the item and then release the button. You use this method to move an item from one area of the computer screen to another.

The Conventions in This Book

A number of typographic and layout styles have been used throughout *Internet Simplified* to distinguish different types of information.

Bold

Bold type represents the names of commands and options that you interact with. Bold type also indicates text and numbers that you must type into a dialog box or window.

Italics

Italic words introduce a new term and are followed by a definition.

Numbered Steps

You must perform the instructions in numbered steps in order to successfully complete a section and achieve the final results.

Bulleted Steps

These steps point out various optional features. You do not have to perform these steps; they simply give additional information about a feature. Steps without bullets tell you what the program does in response to your following a numbered step. For example, if you click a menu command, a dialog box may appear, or a window may open. The step text may also tell you what the final result is when you follow a set of numbered steps.

Notes

Notes give additional information. They may describe special conditions that may occur during an operation. They may warn you of a situation that you want to avoid, for example the loss of data. A note may also cross-reference a related area of the book. A cross-reference may guide you to another chapter, or another section with the current chapter.

 You can easily identify the tips in any section by looking for the Simplify It icon. Tips offer additional information, including tips, hints, and tricks. You can use the tip information to go beyond what you have learned in the steps.

Operating System Difference

The screen shots used in this book were captured using the Windows Vista and Mac OS X 10.5 (Leopard) operating systems. The interface features shown in the tasks may differ slightly if you are using a Windows XP or earlier Windows operating system, or an earlier version of Mac OS X.

Learning Internet Basics

Are you ready to take advantage of the rich diversity of the Internet, whether for education or entertainment? If so, then you need to understand what the Internet is about and what you can do with it.

This chapter helps you do that by introducing you to the Internet. You learn the origins of the Internet and a number of key concepts that will help you understand other topics in the book.

You also learn how the Internet works, the various types of Internet services that are available to you, and what kinds of things you can do on the Internet.

Introducing the Internet

The Internet is a vast, worldwide network that enables you to read the latest news, do research, shop, communicate, listen to music, play games, and access a wide variety of information.

Although the Internet has been popular only since about the mid-1990s, it has been around since the 1960s when it began as an experimental network with just a few participants in the United States. Now, thanks to ocean-spanning cables and satellite access, the Internet is a truly global phenomenon.

Origins

The Internet began in the late 1960s as a research project sponsored by the U.S. Defense Department's Advanced Research Projects Agency (ARPA). The original network — named ARPANET — launched in October 1969 and included just two sites: the Stanford Research Institute (SRI) and the University of California, Los Angeles (UCLA). The name "Internet" was first used in December 1974, and over time the Internet expanded to include other government agencies, universities, research labs, and businesses.

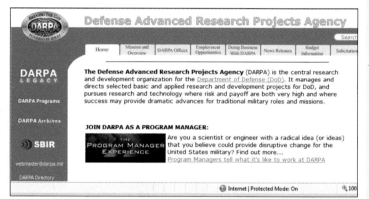

Worldwide Network

You may have a local area network (LAN) where you live or work, so you know that you can use a LAN to work with shared resources on other computers. The Internet is also a network, but on a much vaster scale. The Internet is a worldwide network that enables you to view and share information on other computers around the world.

Backbone

Most Internet data travels along a collection of telephone lines and fiber-optic cables that span the world. This collection of lines and cables makes up the so-called *backbone* of the Internet. Data travels along this backbone at nearly the speed of light, so you can usually access data on the other side of the world in seconds.

Internet Service Provider

In the same way that you need an account with the phone company to make or receive calls, and an account with the cable company to view cable TV, you also need an account to access the Internet. In this case, you set up the account with an Internet service provider (ISP), which is a company that has direct access to the Internet backbone. You use a modem to access an ISP, which then connects you to the Internet.

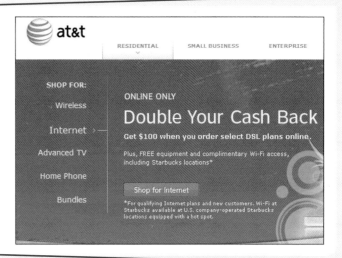

Dial-Up Access

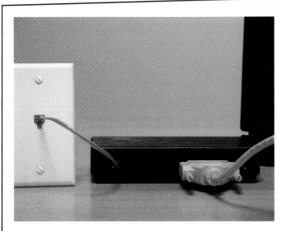

Dial-up Internet access uses a dial-up modem and a telephone line to connect to the Internet. Although dial-up accounts are inexpensive, they are also very slow. You learn more about this and other types of Internet connection in Chapter 2.

Broadband Access

Broadband Internet access uses a high-speed modem to connect to the Internet. The connection is made through a digital subscriber line (DSL) telephone service, television cable hookup, or satellite dish. Broadband accounts are extremely fast, although they are slightly more expensive than dial-up accounts.

Understanding Internet Services

People always talk about *the* Internet, as though it was a single system. That is fine, because it simplifies things. However, you should know that the Internet is actually a collection of several different systems, each of which operates slightly differently.

Each of these systems is called a *service*, and there are four main services that you will use

when you are connected to the Internet: the World Wide Web, e-mail, instant messaging, and media.

There are dozens of other services associated with the Internet, but most are too obscure, too technical, or too outdated to worry about.

The World Wide Web

The World Wide Web is an interlinked collection of data. It is divided into separate *pages*, where each page has information on a specific topic. Most pages have at least one *link* that you can click to take you to a related page. There are billions of Web pages that cover millions of topics. For more information about the Web, see Chapter 3.

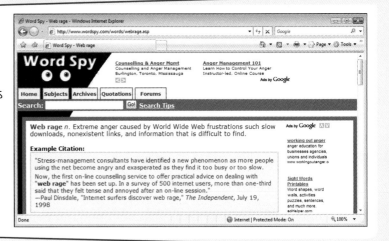

E-mail

You can use electronic mail — most often abbreviated as e-mail — to exchange messages. Your ISP or another company supplies you with an e-mail account, and you use that account to send and receive messages with other Internet users. Unlike postal mail messages which can take days to be delivered and require postage, e-mail messages are usually delivered within minutes and you do not pay an extra charge to send them. For more information about e-mail, see Chapter 10.

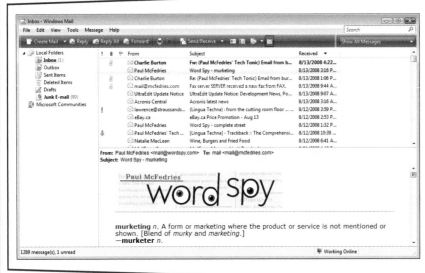

Instant Messaging

You can use instant messaging to send and receive messages. Like e-mail, these are typed messages, but instant messages are exchanged immediately. That is, when you are connected to another person through an instant messaging system, each sent message appears within seconds, so instant messaging is very similar to a conversation. For more information about sending and receiving instant messages, see Chapter 12.

Media

You can use the Internet to play songs and listen to radio stations. You can also run animations, view movie trailers, watch videos, and access many other types of media. The Internet has a few separate media services, but you mostly access media through other services, particularly the World Wide Web. For more information about Internet media, see Chapter 7.

Learn How the Internet Works

To drive a car, you do not need to know how the engine works or understand the principle of internal combustion, but you do need to know the basics of driving so that you can use your vehicle to get to your destination.

The Internet is similar. That is, you do not need to know how the Internet's backbone equipment works or understand the principles of networking, but it does help to know the basics of how data is transferred to get the information you need.

Specifically, you should understand how data gets from Internet sites to your computer.

ISP Connection

Although the Internet is used in many different ways, by far the most common use is for individuals such as you to retrieve data from a remote site. Before you can do this, you must connect your computer to your ISP, which then gives you access to the entire Internet. Data is then transferred over this connection, which might be a phone line, TV cable, or satellite link. For more information on connecting to the Internet, see Chapter 2.

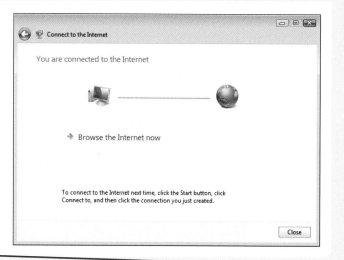

Internet Servers

Almost all the Internet's data is stored on special computers called *servers*. A server's job is to store data, and different servers are configured for different Internet services. For example, a Web server stores World Wide Web data, an incoming e-mail server stores e-mail messages sent to you, and an outgoing e-mail server ensures that messages you send get routed to the correct recipient.

Data Request

When you require data from the Internet, you first open a program designed to work with that data, such as a Web browser, an e-mail program, or instant messaging software. You then use that program to specify the data you want. For example, in your Web browser you might enter the address of a Web page, or in your e-mail program you might run the command to check for new incoming messages. The program then contacts the appropriate server and sends the server a request for the data.

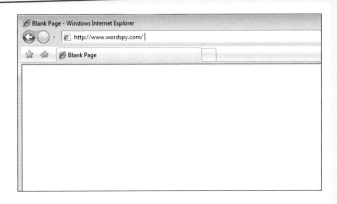

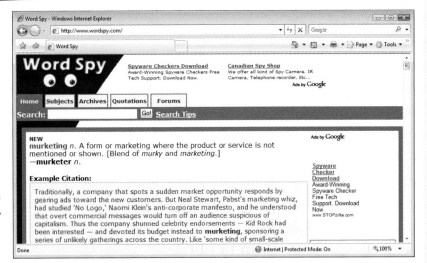

Data Transmission

When an Internet server receives a request for data, it first checks to see if that data exists. If not, the server replies with an error code. For example, if you used your Web browser to request an unknown Web page, the server returns an error code that corresponds to the "File Not Found" error. Otherwise, the server breaks up the data into separate pieces called *packets*, and those packets are sent to your computer.

Data Display

The program you are using — such as a Web browser or e-mail program — waits for the server to respond and then displays the results. If you sent an invalid request, the program displays the error message. For example, if the Web browser receives a "File Not Found" error, it displays that error to you. Otherwise, the program gathers the data packets and, when they are all received, it reassembles the packets and then displays the data.

Discover What You Can Do on the Internet

More than a billion people have access to the Internet, the Web is home to tens of billions of pages, and over one hundred billion e-mail messages are sent each day. With numbers like these, the question is not "What can you do on the Internet," but rather "What can you *not* do on the Internet."

That is, almost anything you can do in the real world has an equivalent in the online world. This includes reading news, researching topics, communicating with other people, making friends, sharing information, buying and selling goods and services, playing games, and listening to or watching media.

Stay Informed

The Web is home to many sites that enable you to read the latest news. For example, most print sources such as newspapers and magazines have Web sites. Also, a number of magazines exist only online, and there are more recent innovations such as Web logs and news feeds, which you will learn about in Chapter 13.

Do Research

You can use the Web's vast resources to research just about any topic you can think of. The Web has information that can help you with a school project, your family history, or a presentation at work. You can search for the data that you need, as described in Chapter 5, or go to specific research sites.

Communicate with Others

You can use various Internet services to communicate with friends, family, colleagues, and clients that you do not often see face to face. You can send e-mail messages and instant messages, you can participate in online forums and discussion groups, and you can even talk to another person using a microphone, your computer's speakers, and even a Web camera.

Socialize with Others

The Web offers many opportunities to socialize, whether you are looking for a friend or a date, or you just want some good conversation. The various social networking sites are excellent places to make friends, and you learn all about them in Chapter 8.

Share Information

You can also use the Web to create and share information. For example, you can create your own Web site by building Web pages and then publishing them on the Web, as described in Chapter 6. You can also share photos as detailed in Chapter 7, and create your own Web log as described in Chapter 13.

Buy and Sell

E-commerce — the online buying and selling of goods and services — is a big part of the Web. You can use Web-based stores to purchase books, theater tickets, and even cars. There are also many sites that enable you to sell or auction your products or household items. See Chapter 9 for more details on Internet-based buying and selling.

Play Games

You can use the Internet to play many different types of online games. You can solve a puzzle, fly a plane, race a car, go on an adventure, play football or baseball, battle aliens, plan a city, play backgammon or checkers, or deal poker.

Play Media

You can use the Internet to play digital media, including music tracks, audio files, radio stations, video files, animations, and movies. You can either copy or purchase the media and store it on your computer, or you can play media directly from a site.

Chapter 2

Getting on the Internet

Unlike radio signals which exist all around you and so can be accessed just by turning on a radio, you cannot access the Internet without a bit of preparation.

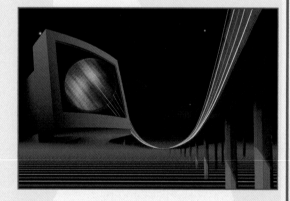

Once you understand how Internet connections work, you need to choose an Internet service provider (ISP) that suits your needs. With your account activated, the ISP will send you the information you need to make an Internet connection.

From here, you either set up your network to make the Internet connection, or you use a computer to make the Internet connection directly.

This chapter takes you through the details of each of these steps.

Choose an Internet Service Provider

To connect to the Internet, you must sign up for an account with an Internet service provider. However, there may be dozens of ISPs in your area, so how do you choose the right one?

Choosing an ISP is a matter of doing your homework and comparing various features. The most important of these features is the monthly fee, although remember to take into account the connection type and speed, and compare the different plans each ISP offers.

You also need to consider the number of e-mail accounts the ISP provides, software and hardware offered by the ISP, and extra features such as technical support and contract requirements.

Connection Charges

An ISP charges you a monthly fee, which can range from a few dollars to $40 or $50 per month. What you pay depends on the connection speed and how many minutes of connection time (or how many gigabytes of data transfer, which is called *bandwidth*) you are allowed each month. Keep in mind that a few ISPs still charge an extra fee per hour if you exceed your allotted time (or per gigabyte if you exceed your bandwidth limit). To avoid extra fees, you may want to consider unlimited Internet access, which is offered by almost all ISPs.

Connection Speed

Internet connections have different speeds, and these speeds determine how fast the Internet data is sent to your computer. If you connect to your ISP using a modem, the connection speed will likely be up to 56 kilobits per second. You can obtain high-speed (or *broadband*) connections through a TV cable, a digital subscriber line (DSL) phone line, or a satellite link. Most broadband connections offer speeds of over 1,000 kilobits per second, or 1 megabit per second.

Download versus Upload

When researching the connection speed offered by an ISP, bear in mind that you will often see two different speeds listed: download and upload. The *download speed* (also called the *downstream speed*) is the rate at which Internet data is sent to your computer; the *upload speed* (also called the *upstream speed*) is the rate at which data from your computer is sent to the Internet. Most data is downloaded, so the download speed is the most important.

Connection Plans

All major ISPs offer a number of connection plans. These typically feature cheaper plans that offer slower connection speeds and fewer features, to more expensive plans that offer the fastest speeds and lots of extras. A good ISP will offer a comparison page that enables you to make side-by-side comparisons of the different plans to see which one is right for you.

E-mail Accounts

Almost every Internet account comes with at least one e-mail account, but most offer multiple e-mail accounts, which is important if you want to provide e-mail to other members of your family. Be sure to check the total number of e-mail accounts you get with each ISP. It is also important to check the maximum amount of data you can store with each e-mail account.

Software

Many ISPs offer one or more software programs free with each account. These are usually security programs that help keep you safe while connected to the Internet. Typical software includes an anti-virus program, an anti-spam program, a utility that blocks pop-up ads, and a program that enables you to control your children's access to the Internet.

Hardware

All broadband ISPs can supply you with a broadband modem. You can usually purchase the modem outright, or you can rent the modem for a few dollars a month. Larger ISPs often offer the modem free when you sign up for one of the more expensive accounts. Such accounts also sometimes come with a free router (also called a *gateway*), which is a network device that connects to the Internet, and your network computers access the Internet through the router.

Other Features

Check the details of each Internet plan to see what other features you get. The most important of these are customer service and technical support, which should be free and have convenient hours. Another important consideration is whether the ISP requires you to sign a contract. Most ISPs let you pay month-to-month, but some require commitments of a year or more. If you want to put up your own Web site, see if the ISP offers free access to their Web server.

Explore Internet Connections

Before you connect to the Internet, you need to know how to set up your modem.

A *modem* is a device that receives data from the Internet and sends data from your computer to the Internet. There are two main types of modem: a dialup modem and a broadband modem.

You use a dialup modem if you have a dialup account with an ISP. Note that most ISPs do not provide the dialup modem, so you must purchase it yourself.

You use a broadband modem if you have a broadband account with an ISP. In most cases, the ISP will provide you with the broadband modem, which you can purchase or rent.

Connect a Dial-Up Modem

Serial or USB Cable

You use a cable to attach the modem to your computer. If the modem requires a serial cable, run the cable from the modem's serial port to the serial port in the back of your computer. If the modem requires a USB cable, run the cable from the modem's USB port to a free USB port on your computer. Note that you do not need to perform this step if your modem resides inside your computer case.

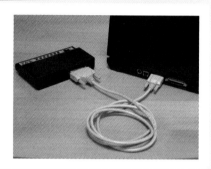

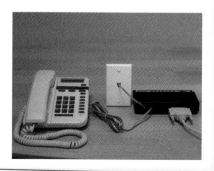

Phone Line

Examine the back of your modem and look for a jack that fits a regular telephone cable. In particular, look for a jack labeled *Line*. Note that some modems label this jack with *Telco*, or they show a picture of a wall jack instead of a label. Run a phone cord from the wall jack and plug it into the modem's Line jack.

Telephone Connection

The back of your modem should have a second jack that fits a regular telephone cable. On most modems, this jack is labeled *Phone*, although some modems show a graphic of a telephone, instead. Run a second phone cord from your telephone to the Phone jack. This enables you to use the phone when you are not using your modem.

Connect a Broadband Modem

Phone Connection

Look on the back of the broadband modem for a port labeled *DSL* (or sometimes *ADSL*). Run a phone cable from the wall jack to the DSL port on the modem. Note, too, that many ISPs require that you install a phone filter device to reduce the noise created by the DSL signal. Attach a splitter and then run a phone cable from the splitter to the Line port on the phone filter, and run a second phone cable from the Phone port on the filter to your telephone.

Cable Connection

If you have a broadband account with the cable company, look on the back of your broadband modem for a port labeled *Cable*. Run a TV cable from the wall jack to the Cable port on the modem. Note that many ISPs insist that you register the broadband modem by accessing a page on the ISP's Web site and sometimes entering a code or the serial number of the modem. Check with your ISP to see if you need to do this.

Direct Connection

If your computer is the only one accessing the Internet, you can connect it directly to the broadband modem. The back of the modem should contain two other ports, one labeled *Ethernet* and one labeled *USB*. If you have a network card inside your computer and a network cable, run the cable from the modem's Ethernet port to the network card port. Otherwise, run a USB cable from the modem's USB port to a free USB port on your computer.

Router Connection

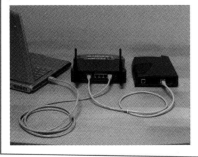

If you have a network and you want each computer on the network to access the same Internet connection, then you need to add a router (also called a *gateway*) to your network. Run a network cable from the modem's Ethernet port to the port labeled *WAN* (or sometimes *Internet*) on the back of the router. Then run network cables from each computer to the router's network ports. If the router supports wireless, you can also connect computers wirelessly.

Configure Your Router to Connect to the Internet

You can use a router to share a broadband Internet connection with the other computers on your network. However, for this to work properly, you must configure the router to connect to your ISP.

Some ISPs provide software that performs this configuration for you. If you do not have such software, then you must perform the configuration by hand. To do this in most cases, you need several pieces of information: the address of the router; the user name and password for the router; and the type of Internet connection — usually either Dynamic (or DHCP) or PPPoE. For the latter, you also need your account's user name and password.

Configure Your Router to Connect to the Internet

CONFIGURE THE CONNECTION

① In a Web browser, type the address of the router and press Enter.

Note: See your router's documentation to learn its address (which may be called its IP address).

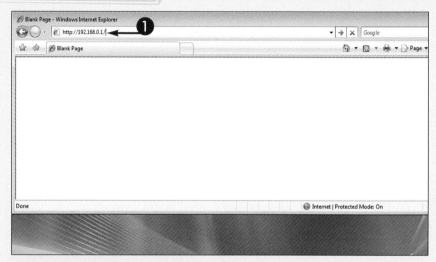

The router prompts you for a user name and password.

② Use the **User Name** text box to type the router's user name.

③ Use the **Password** text box to type the router's password.

Note: See your router's documentation to learn its default user name and password.

④ Click **Log In**.

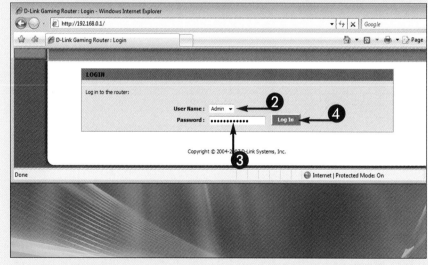

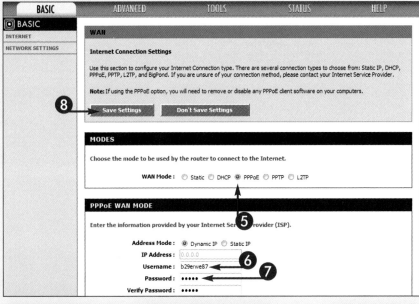

The router's setup pages appear.

Note: The layout of the setup pages varies from router to router. The steps that follow are typical for most D-Link routers.

⑤ Click the Internet connection type (◉ changes to ◉).

Note: See your ISP kit to learn which type you need to choose.

⑥ Type your user name.

⑦ Type your password.

⑧ Click to save your settings.

CHECK THE CONNECTION STATUS

① Click **Status**.

● Check that the status says **Connected**.

What do I do if the router status shows as Disconnected?
After you have configured the router with your connection data, the router should make the connection automatically and keep the connection on. If the connection is off, access the status page. If you are using a PPPoE connection, click **Connect**; if you are using a DHCP connection, click **DHCP Release** and then click **DHCP Renew**.

Should I change my router's default user name and password?
Yes, as soon as possible. Most routers come with well-known user names such as *Admin* and well-known passwords such as *password*, so it is easy for another person to connect to your router, particularly if it includes a wireless access point. Log on to the router and locate the status page that enables you to change the user name and password.

Start the Connect to the Internet Wizard

In Windows Vista, you can use the Connect to the Internet wizard to help you connect to the Internet. The wizard guides you through a step-by-step process. This is much easier than trying to set up the connection on your own.

With the Connect to the Internet wizard, you can set up three types of Internet connection:

dialup, broadband, and wireless. This section shows you how to start the wizard, and the following sections show you how to set up each type.

Note that you do not need to follow these instructions if you have configured your router to connect to the Internet.

Start the Connect to the Internet Wizard

① Click **Start** (🔘).

② Click **Connect To**.

The Connect to a network dialog box appears.

③ Click the **Set up a connection or network** link.

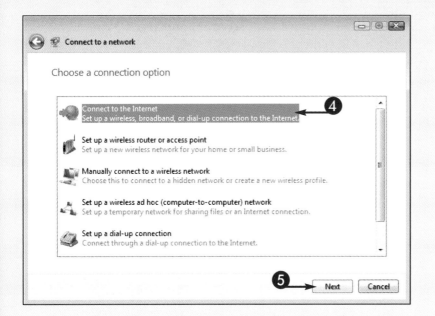

The Choose a connection option dialog box appears.

④ Click **Connect to the Internet**.

⑤ Click **Next**.

The Connect to the Internet wizard appears.

The following sections take you through the specific steps for creating dialup, broadband, and wireless Internet connections.

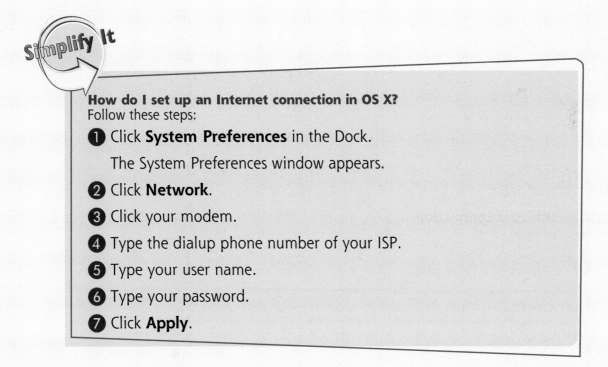

How do I set up an Internet connection in OS X?
Follow these steps:

❶ Click **System Preferences** in the Dock.

The System Preferences window appears.

❷ Click **Network**.

❸ Click your modem.

❹ Type the dialup phone number of your ISP.

❺ Type your user name.

❻ Type your password.

❼ Click **Apply**.

Set Up a Dialup Internet Connection

If your computer comes with an internal or external modem, you can use that modem to establish a dialup Internet connection through your Internet service provider.

If your computer has an external modem, make sure the modem is turned on before setting up the connection. Also, make sure that the phone and the serial or USB cables are connected as described earlier in this chapter in the "Explore Internet Connections" section.

To configure the dialup connection, you need to know your ISP's dialup phone number, as well as the user name and password for your Internet account.

Set Up a Dialup Internet Connection

① Display the Connect to the Internet wizard, as described earlier in the section "Start the Connect to the Internet Wizard."

② Click **Dial-up**.

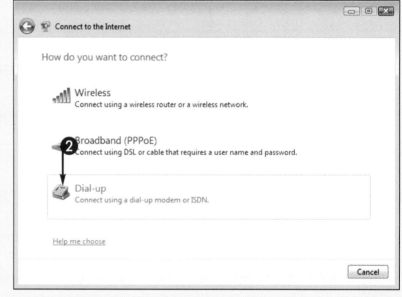

The wizard asks for the connection information from your ISP.

③ Type your ISP's dialup phone number.

④ Type your Internet account's user name.

⑤ Type your Internet account's password.

● If you want to avoid having to type your password each time you connect, you can select the **Remember this password** check box (☐ changes to ☑).

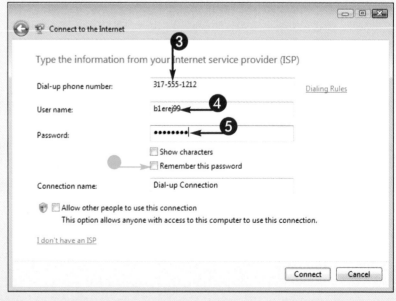

Connect to the Internet

Type the information from your Internet service provider (ISP)

Dial-up phone number: 317-555-1212   Dialing Rules

User name: b1erej99

Password: ••••••••

☐ Show characters
☐ Remember this password

Connection name: Dial-up Connection

☐ Allow other people to use this connection
This option allows anyone with access to this computer to use this connection.

I don't have an ISP

6 → Connect   Cancel

Connect to the Internet

You are connected to the Internet

Browse the Internet now

To connect to the Internet next time, click the Start button, click
Connect to, and then click the connection you just created.

● To make this connection available to other people who use your computer, you can select the **Allow other people to use this connection** check box (☐ changes to ☑).

6 Click **Connect**.

Windows Vista creates and then tests the connection.

● If the test is successful, you can click **Browse the Internet now** to open the Web browser.

Note: See Chapter 3 to learn more about Web browsing.

7 Click **Close** at the bottom of the window (not shown).

Note: See the section "Connect to the Internet" to learn how to connect to the Internet again in the future.

Simplify It

Can I make or receive a phone call while I am using my dialup Internet connection?
No, it is not possible to place outgoing calls or receive incoming calls while your dialup Internet connection is active. A dialup connection just uses a regular phone line connection, so being connected to the Internet is no different than being on a phone call. Note, too, that if you have call waiting it can interrupt the Internet connection, so turn off call waiting before dialing.

My area requires 10-digit dialing. How do I handle this?
When you type the phone number for the ISP, add the area code in front of the phone number. For example, if the area code is 317 and the phone number is 555-1234, type **317-555-1234**.

Set Up a Broadband Internet Connection

If you have signed up for a PPPoE broadband account with your ISP, you can use that account to access the Internet either through a network router or directly through your computer. To use the connection directly, you need to provide Windows Vista with the user name and password for that account.

Your ISP should provide a broadband modem when you sign up your account. Make sure that modem is turned on and connected as described in the "Explore Internet Connections" section.

Set Up a Broadband Internet Connection

1 Display the Connect to the Internet wizard, as described earlier in the section "Start the Connect to the Internet Wizard."

2 Click **Broadband (PPPoE)**.

The wizard asks for the connection information from your ISP.

3 Type your Internet account's user name.

4 Type your Internet account's password.

● If you want to avoid having to type your password each time you connect, you can select the **Remember this password** check box (☐ changes to ☑).

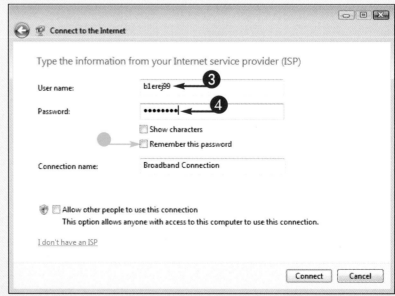

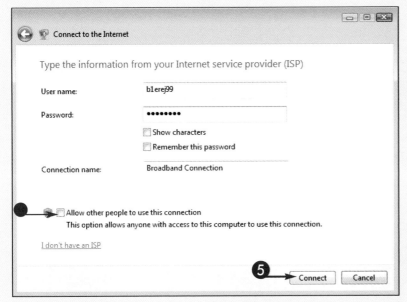

Type the information from your Internet service provider (ISP)

User name: b1erej99

Password: ••••••••

☐ Show characters
☐ Remember this password

Connection name: Broadband Connection

☐ Allow other people to use this connection
This option allows anyone with access to this computer to use this connection.

I don't have an ISP

⑤ ⟶ Connect   Cancel

Connect to the Internet

You are connected to the Internet

● ⟶ Browse the Internet now

● To make this connection available to other people who use your computer, you can select the **Allow other people to use this connection** check box (☐ changes to ☑).

⑤ Click **Connect**.

Windows Vista creates and then tests the connection.

● If the test is successful, you can click **Browse the Internet now** to open the Web browser. See Chapter 3 to learn more about Web browsing.

⑥ Click **Close** at the bottom of the window (not shown).

Note: See the section "Connect to the Internet" to learn how to connect to the Internet again in the future.

Simplify It

Do I have to get my broadband modem from my ISP?
No, not in most cases. Some ISPs put together Internet connection kits that include the broadband modem and configuration software, and they make those kits available in retail stores for purchase. You can also purchase stand-alone broadband modems, although in this case you probably need to contact the ISP and provide them with the serial number of the modem.

Do I need to go through these steps if my ISP uses a dynamic (DCHP) connection?
No, these steps are valid only for a PPPoE (Point-to-Point Protocol over Ethernet) broadband connection, which is typically associated with DSL accounts. If you have a DHCP (Dynamic Host Control Protocol) Internet connection — as is the case with most cable broadband accounts — then Windows should have access to the Internet without any configuration.

Set Up a Wireless Internet Connection

If you have a broadband modem attached to a router that also includes a wireless access point, you can set up a wireless connection to the router. This enables you to access the Internet through the router without having to make a physical connection to the router.

To connect to a wireless access point, you need to know the network name that the access point is using. Also, most wireless access points have security enabled, so to connect to the network you must know the correct password or security key.

Set Up a Wireless Internet Connection

1 Display the Connect to the Internet wizard.

Note: To connect to the Internet wizard, follow steps **1** to **5** in the section "Start the Connect to the Internet Wizard."

2 Click **Wireless**.

The Connect to the Internet wizard displays a list of available wireless networks.

3 Click your wireless network.

4 Click **Connect**.

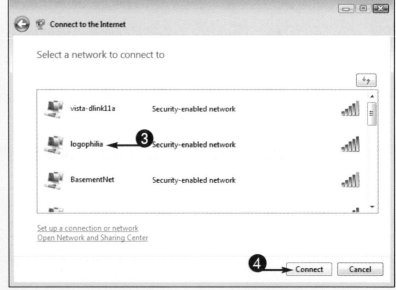

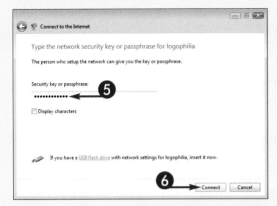

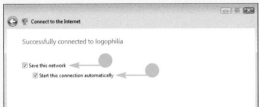

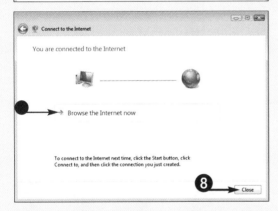

If your network is protected by a security key, the Connect to the Internet wizard prompts you to type that key. See the person who configured your network to obtain the security key.

5 Type the network's security key.

6 Click **Connect**.

The Connect to the Internet wizard connects to the wireless network.

● You can leave these check boxes selected and Windows Vista connects you to the network automatically each time it is within range.

7 Click **Next** at the bottom of the window (not shown).

Windows Vista tests the Internet connection.

● If the test is successful, you can click **Browse the Internet now** to open the Web browser.

Note: *See Chapter 3 to learn more about Web browsing.*

8 Click **Close**.

How do I make a wireless Internet connection in OS X?
Follow these steps:

① Click the **AirPort Status** icon (🛜).

② If you see your network in the list, click it; otherwise, click **Other**.

③ Type your network name, if necessary.

④ Click ⬧ and then click the type of security your network uses.

⑤ Type your network password.

⑥ Click **OK**.

Connect to the Internet

Once you configure your Internet account, you can use it to connect to the Internet without having to go through the Connect to the Internet wizard each time.

In most cases, you need to enter your connection data each time you connect. For example, for a dialup or PPPoE broadband account, you must enter your user name and password. For a wireless connection, you must enter the security key.

However, if you selected the Remember this password check box for a dialup or broadband connection, or if you left the options for automatic wireless connections selected, Windows Vista connects you to the Internet without prompting you for information.

Connect to the Internet

① Click **Start** (⊞).

② Click **Connect To**.

The Connect to a network dialog box appears.

③ Click the Internet connection you want to use.

④ Click **Connect**.

If prompted, type the connection data, such as the account password or wireless security key.

Windows Vista connects to the Internet.

● The ⊠ icon appears when the connection is active.

In OS X, click ⌘, click **System Preferences**, and then click **Network**. Click your modem and then click **Connect**.

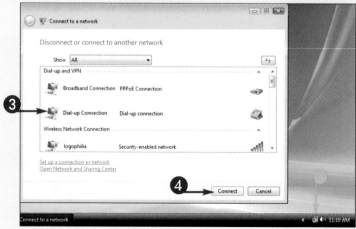

Disconnect from the Internet

After you complete your Internet session, you should disconnect to avoid exceeding your allotted connection time. This does not apply to most broadband and wireless connections.

Some ISPs allow you a specified connection time per month, and they charge you a fee for each minute that you exceed your allotted

time. Therefore, you should always disconnect when you finish to avoid additional connection charges.

Remember, too, that if you are using a dialup connection, you cannot use the telephone while the connection is active, so you must disconnect if you need to make or receive a call.

Disconnect from the Internet

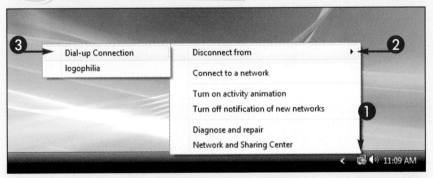

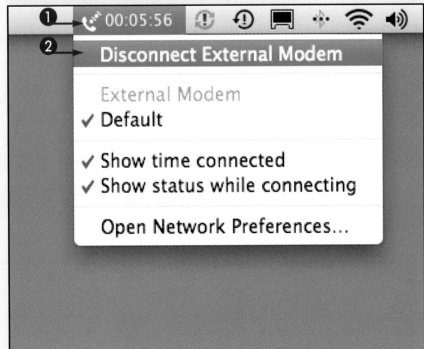

WINDOWS VISTA

1 Right-click the connection icon (⬜).

2 Click **Disconnect from**.

3 Click the Internet connection you want to disconnect.

Windows Vista disconnects from the Internet.

OS X

1 Click the **Modem Status** icon (⬜).

Note: If you do not see the Modem Status icon, click ⬜, click System Preferences, and then click Network. Click your modem and then click Show modem status in the menu bar (⬜ changes to ☑).

2 Click **Disconnect** *Modem* (where *Modem* is the name of your modem).

OS X disconnects from the Internet.

Make Your Internet Connection More Secure

When your computer is connected to the Internet, it is possible for another person on the Internet to access your computer and infect it with a virus or cause other damage. You can turn on the Windows Vista Firewall, which prevents intruders from accessing your computer while you are connected to the Internet.

The Windows Vista Firewall is usually turned on by default. However, the firewall is so important that it is worth checking to make sure it is turned on.

Make Your Internet Connection More Secure

① Click **Start** (🔲).

② Type **windows firewall**.

③ Click **Windows Firewall** in the search results.

You can also click **Start** (🔲), click **Control Panel**, and then click **Check this computer's security status**.

The Windows Security Center window appears.

④ Check the Firewall status.

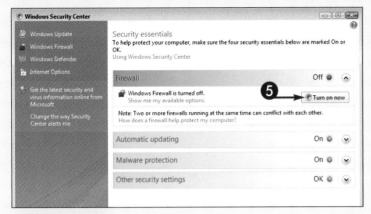

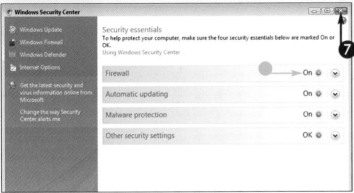

⑤ If the Firewall setting is Off, click **Turn on now**.

⑥ If you see the User Account Control dialog box, click **Continue** or type an administrator's password and then click **Submit**.

● In the Windows Security Center window, the Firewall setting changes to On.

⑦ Click **Close** (▣) to close the Windows Security Center window.

Simplify It

How do I activate the OS X Firewall?
Follow these steps:

❶ Click ⌘.

❷ Click **System Preferences**.

The System Preferences window appears.

❸ Click **Security**.

The Security pane appears.

❹ Click **Firewall**.

❺ Click **Allow only essential services**.

❻ Click **Advanced**.

❼ Click **Enable Stealth Mode** (☐ changes to ☑).

❽ Click **OK**.

Chapter 3

Browsing the World Wide Web

After you set up your Internet connection, you can use Internet Explorer, Firefox, Safari, or another browser program to navigate, or *surf*, the sites on the World Wide Web.

You will probably find that you spend the majority of your online time browsing the Web. That is not surprising because the Web is useful, entertaining, fun, interesting, and provocative.

This chapter introduces you to the Web, takes you through the basics of browsing sites, and shows you standard Web techniques such as saving your favorite sites, downloading files, and filling in forms.

The next few chapters expand your Web knowledge by telling you about Web security, the ins and outs of searching, and how to get things done on the Web.

Introducing the World Wide Web

The World Wide Web, or simply the Web, is a massive storehouse of information that resides on computers, called *Web servers*, located all over the world.

Each Web server hosts one or more Web sites, and each of those sites contains dozens, hundreds, or even thousands of documents called *pages*.

You navigate from site to site and from page to page by clicking special words, phrases, or images called *links*, or by entering the address of the site or page you want to view. You do all of this using a special software program called a *Web browser*.

Web Page

World Wide Web information is presented on Web pages that you download to your computer using a Web browser program, such as Internet Explorer. Each Web page can combine text with images, sounds, music, and even videos to present information on a particular subject. The Web consists of billions of pages covering almost every imaginable topic.

Web Site

A Web site (sometimes spelled as Website) is a collection of Web pages associated with a particular person, business, government, school, or organization. Some Web sites deal with only a single topic, but most sites contain pages on a variety of topics. Almost all Web sites are available free to any person, but a few sites require either a password or a paid subscription to access the content.

Web Server

Web sites are stored on a Web server, which is a special computer that makes Web pages available for people to browse. A Web server is usually a powerful computer capable of handling thousands of site visitors at a time. The largest Web sites are run by *server farms*, which are networks that may contain dozens, hundreds, or even thousands of servers.

Web Browser

A Web browser is a software program designed to navigate, download, and display Web pages. Your operating system ships with a Web browser — Windows Vista comes with Internet Explorer 7 and Mac OS X comes with Safari — but you can download other Web browsers, such as Firefox.

Links

A link is a kind of cross-reference to another Web page. A text link usually appears underlined and in a different color from the regular text on the page. A link can also appear as an image. When you click the link, the other page loads into your Web browser automatically. The link can take you to another page on the same site or to a page on another Web site.

Web Address

Every Web site and Web page has its own Web address that uniquely identifies the page. This address is called the Uniform Resource Locator, or URL (pronounced *yoo-ar-ell* or *erl*). If you know the address of a page, you can type that address into your Web browser to view the page.

URL

The URL of a Web site or page is composed of several parts. All URLs include at least the *transfer method* (usually http, which stands for HyperText Transfer Protocol) and the *Web site domain name*. Many URLs also include the *directory* where the Web page is located on the server and the *Web page filename*.

The Web site domain name most often uses the .com (business) suffix, but other common suffixes include .gov (government), .org (nonprofit organization), and country domains such as .ca (Canada) and .uk (United Kingdom).

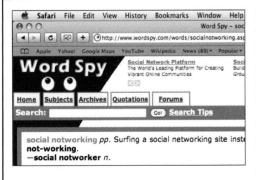

Understanding Web Browsing Basics

Almost all Web pages include links to other pages that contain information related to something in the current page, and you can use these links to navigate to other Web pages. When you click a link, your Web browser loads the other page.

Knowing which words, phrases, or images are links is not always obvious. The only way to tell for sure in many cases is to position the ⇖ over the text or image; if the ⇖ changes to ⛶, you are dealing with a link.

Alternatively, if you know the address of a specific Web page, you can type it into the Web browser and the program displays the page.

Understanding Web Browsing Basics

CLICK A LINK

① Position the ⇖ over the link (⇖ changes to ⛶).

② Click the text or image.

● The status bar shows the current download status.

Note: *The address shown in the Status bar when you point at a link may be different from the one shown when the page is downloading. This happens when the Web site "redirects" the link, which happens frequently.*

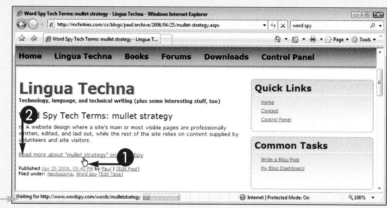

The linked Web page appears.

● The Web page title and address change after the linked page is loaded.

● The status bar shows Done when the page is completely loaded.

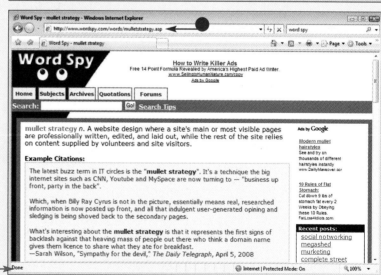

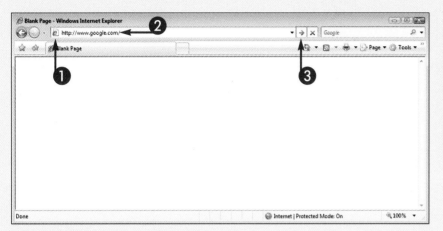

ENTER A WEB PAGE ADDRESS

① Click inside the address bar.

② Type the address of the Web page.

③ Click the right arrow icon (☐).

The Web page appears.

● The Web page title changes after the page is loaded.

● You can click **Back** (☐) to return to a previously visited page.

Are there any shortcuts I can use to enter Web page addresses?
Here are some useful keyboard techniques:

● After you finish typing the address, press `Enter` instead of clicking ☐.

● Most Web addresses begin with *http://*. You can leave off these characters when you type your address; the Web browser adds them automatically.

● If the address uses the form http://www. *something*.com, type just the *something* part and press `Ctrl` + `Enter` (or ⌘ + `Return` on a Mac). The browser automatically adds *http:// www.* at the beginning and *.com* at the end.

When I try to load a page, why does the browser tell me that "The page cannot be displayed"?
This message means that the browser is unable to contact a Web server at the address you typed. This is often a temporary glitch, so run the browser's Reload command to try loading the page again. If the trouble persists, make sure you are connected to the Internet, and then double-check your address to ensure that you typed it correctly. If you did, the site may be unavailable for some reason. Try again in a few hours.

Learn About Internet Explorer

If your computer is running Windows, then your default Web browser is most likely Internet Explorer. This is Microsoft's browser, and it comes with all versions of Windows, which is part of the reason why it is the most popular browser in use today.

This section introduces you to the main features of the Internet Explorer window, and shows you how to use those features to navigate Web pages. You also learn how to change the Internet Explorer home page, which is the page that appears when you first start Internet Explorer.

Back
Click this button to return to a page you visited previously in the current browsing session.

Forward
After you click Back to return to a previous page, you can click Forward to reverse course and move forward through your visited pages.

Recent Pages
Click this arrow to see a list of the pages you have visited during the current browsing session. You can then click a page to return to it.

Address List
Click this arrow to display a list of addresses you have typed into the address bar. Click an address to surf to that page.

Refresh
Click this button to reload the current page. You can also reload the current page by pressing **F5**.

Home
Click this button to return to the Internet Explorer home page. You can also return to the home page by pressing **Alt** + **M**.

Search
Use this box to search for information. Click inside the box, type a word or phrase, and then press **Enter**.

Change the Home Page

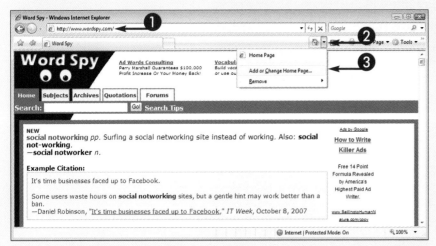

1 Display the Web page that you want to use as your home page.

2 Click ⊡ beside the **Home** icon (🏠).

3 Click **Add or Change Home Page**.

The Change Home Page dialog box appears.

4 Click **Use this webpage as your only home page** (◎ changes to ◉).

5 Click **Yes**.

Internet Explorer changes your home page.

You can click 🏠 to display the home page at any time.

Can I have more than one home page in Internet Explorer?
Yes, you can specify multiple home pages, and Internet Explorer will load each one automatically whenever you start the program. Each page appears in its own tab (see "Browse Multiple Web Sites Using Tabs"). Follow steps **1** to **3**, click **Add this webpage to your home page tabs** (◎ changes to ◉), and then click **Yes**.

Can I get Internet Explorer to load without displaying a home page?
Yes, you can configure Internet Explorer to load a blank page, which enables the program to open much faster. Click **Tools** and then click **Internet Options** to open the Internet Options dialog box. Click the **General** tab. In the Home page section, click **Use blank**. Click **OK** to put the new setting into effect.

Discover Firefox

If you use Windows or Mac OS X, you can download and install the Firefox Web browser. Firefox is a free program that is used by millions of people because it is fast and easy to use.

This section introduces you to the main features of the Firefox window, and shows you how to use those features to navigate Web pages. You also learn how to change the Firefox home page, which is the page that appears when you first start the program.

Back
Click this button to return to a page you visited previously in the current browsing session.

Forward
After you click Back to return to a previous page, you can click Forward to reverse course and move forward through your visited pages.

Recent Pages
Click this arrow to see a list of the pages you have visited during the current browsing session. You can then click a page to return to it.

Reload
Click this button to reload the current page. You can also reload the current page by pressing Ctrl + R (or ⌘ + R in Mac OS X).

Home
Click this button to return to the Firefox home page. You can also return to the home page by pressing Alt + Home (or Shift + ⌘ + H in Mac OS X).

Address List
Click this arrow to display a list of addresses you have typed into the address bar. Click an address to surf to that page.

Search
Use this box to search for information. Click inside the box, type a word or phrase, and then press Enter.

Change the Home Page

① Display the Web page that you want to use as your home page.

② Click **Tools**.

③ Click **Options**.

Note: *In Mac OS X, click* ***Firefox*** *and then click* ***Preferences***, *instead.*

The Options dialog box appears.

④ Click the **Main** tab.

⑤ Click **Use Current Page**.

⑥ Click **OK**.

Firefox changes your home page.

You can click ⌂ to display the home page at any time.

How do I get Firefox?
To get Firefox, go to the Mozilla download page at www.mozilla.org/download.html, click **Firefox**, and then click the **Download** link. If you are using Internet Explorer, click **Run** in the Security Warning dialog box and then follow the installation instructions that appear after the file has downloaded. In Mac OS X, wait until the file has downloaded, and then drag the Firefox icon into your Applications folder.

Can I get Firefox to load without displaying a home page?
Yes, you can configure Firefox to show a blank page at startup for faster loading. Follow steps **1** to **4** to open the Options dialog box and display the Main tab. In the When Firefox Starts list, click ▾ and then click **Show a blank page**. Click **OK** to put the new setting into effect.

Browse with Safari

If you are using a Mac, then your default Web browser is most likely Safari. This is Apple's browser, and it comes with all versions of Mac OS X. If you use Windows, you can download and install the Windows version of Safari.

This section introduces you to the main features of the Safari window, and shows you how to use those features to navigate Web pages. You also learn how to change the Safari home page, which is the page that appears when you first start the program.

Back

Click this button to return to a page you visited previously in the current browsing session.

Forward

After you click Back to return to a previous page, you can click Forward to reverse course and move forward through your visited pages.

Reload

Click this button to reload the current page. You can also reload the current page by pressing ⌘ + R (or Ctrl + R in Windows).

SnapBack

In the address bar, click this icon (⊙) to jump to the top level of the current Web site. In the Search box, click this icon to rerun the most recent search.

Recent Searches

Click this icon (Q▾) to see a list of the pages you have visited during the current browsing session. You can then click a page to return to it.

Search

Use this box to search for information. Click inside the box, type a word or phrase, and then press Return.

Change the Home Page

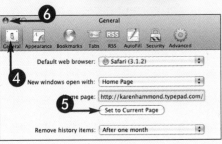

① Display the Web page that you want to use as your home page.

② Click **Safari**.

③ Click **Preferences**.

Note: In Windows, click **Edit** *and then click* **Preferences**, *instead.*

The Safari preferences appear.

④ Click the **General** tab.

⑤ Click **Set to Current Page**.

⑥ Click **Close** (◉).

Safari changes your home page.

You can click **History** and then click **Home** (or press Shift + ⌘ + H) to display the home page at any time.

How do I get Safari for Windows?
To get Safari for Windows, go to the Safari download page at www.apple.com/safari/download, and then click the **Download Safari** link. If you are using Internet Explorer, click **Run** in the Security Warning dialog box and then follow the installation instructions that appear after the file has downloaded. In Firefox, click **Save File**, wait until the file has downloaded, double-click the file, and then click **OK**.

Can I get Safari to load without displaying a home page?
Yes, you can configure Firefox to show a blank page at startup for faster loading. Follow steps **1** to **4** to open the Safari preferences and display the General tab. In the **Home page** text box, delete the current home page, and then click **Close** (◉) to put the new setting into effect.

Browse Multiple Web Sites Using Tabs

You can make it easier to work with multiple Web sites simultaneously by opening each page in its own tab.

When you use a Web browser normally, each page appears in the main part of the browser window, which is usually called the content area. A tab is like a second content area, and it appears "behind" the first one, with only a

small tab (hence the name) visible. Click the tab and you see the second content area and its loaded Web page.

You can open as many pages as you like in their own tabs. This is convenient because all the pages appear within a single Web browser window.

Browse Multiple Web Sites Using Tabs

OPEN A LINK IN A TAB

1 Right-click the link you want to open.

2 Click **Open in New Tab**.

Note: In Firefox or Safari, right-click (or `Control`*-click on a Mac) the link and then click* **Open Link in New Tab***.*

Note: You can also hold down `Ctrl` *(or ⌘ on a Mac) and click the link to open it in a new tab.*

● A new tab appears with the page title.

3 Click the tab to display the page.

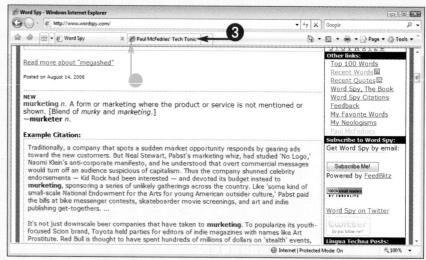

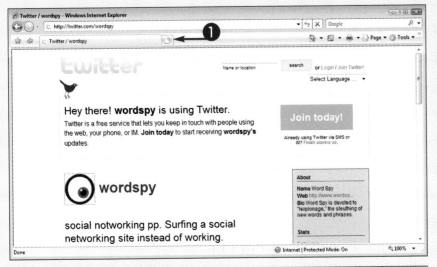

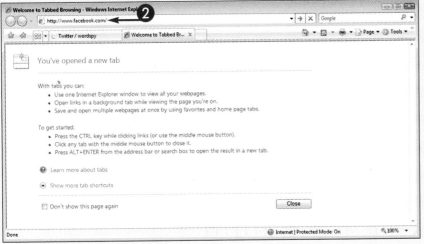

OPEN A WEB PAGE IN A TAB

1 Click the **New Tab** icon ().

Note: In Firefox or Safari, click ***File*** *and then click* ***New Tab***.

Note: You can also press `Ctrl` + `T` *(or ⌘ +* `T` *on a Mac).*

The browser displays a new tab.

2 Type the address of the Web page.

3 Press `Enter`.

The browser loads the page into the new tab.

Simplify It

Is there a way that I can open a link in a new tab and have the browser display the new tab automatically?
Yes, there is. By default, the Web browser opens the new tab, and it leaves the tab in the background so you can continue reading the current page. If you want to read the new page right away, you can force the browser to display the new tab. Hold down the `Ctrl` key (or the ⌘ key in Mac OS X) and click the link.

How do I close a tab that I no longer need?
The easiest way to close a tab is to click the **Close Tab** icon (X) that appears on the right side of each tab in Internet Explorer and Firefox, and on the left side of each tab in Safari. (You can also press `Ctrl` + `W` or ⌘ + `W`.) If you prefer to leave only the current tab open and close all the other open tabs, right-click (or `Control`-click on a Mac) the current tab and then click **Close Other Tabs**.

Fill In a Web Form

If a Web site requires information from you, it presents a page that includes a *Web form*. A form is similar to a dialog box in that it consists of two or more controls that you use to enter or choose information. You then send the form data by clicking a button, which is equivalent to clicking an OK button in a dialog box. The form data is sent to a server computer which processes the data.

One common use for a form is to log in to a restricted Web site, and you use a form to specify your user name and password. You also use Web forms to work with online shopping carts, complete polls or surveys, register for a site or event, and more.

Common Form Controls

Text Box

You use a text box to enter text. Most text boxes use only a single line, but you may also see multi-line boxes called *text areas*.

Password Box

You use a password box to type a password. The characters you type appear as dots for security.

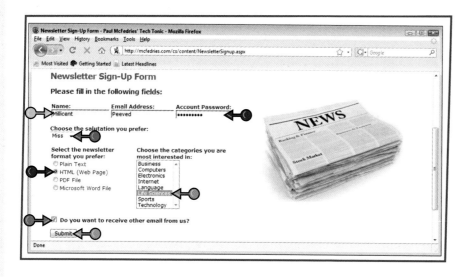

Drop-Down List

A drop-down list displays only one item at a time, and you use the list to select an item. Click ⬛ to drop down the list, and then click the item you want to select.

Selection List

A selection list displays multiple items at a time, and you use a selection list to select an item. In most selection lists you can select only one item, but some lists enable you to select two or more items.

Radio Button

You use radio buttons to select one choice out of several.

Check Box

You use a check box to toggle an option on and off.

Submit Button

You click the submit button to send the form data to the server.

46

Working with Forms

Save Passwords

When you type a password in a form and then submit the form, your Web browser will likely ask if you want it to save the password. This is convenient because it means you do not have to enter the password again the next time you use the form. However, it is also dangerous because it may allow another person who uses your computer to access the site. Avoid saving passwords for sensitive sites such as online banking and corporate pages.

Mandatory Fields

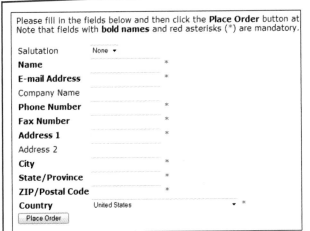

In most forms, you do not have to enter or select data in every field. For example, if a form asks for personal information such as your address, phone number, or birth date, you can (and should) leave such fields blank. However, many forms have at least one field that is required. For example, if you are registering for a site, a user name and password are mandatory. In such cases, the form usually indicates the mandatory fields, often with an asterisk or other symbol.

Form Security

Some form submissions contain sensitive data. For example, when you submit a site login form, the data contains your user name and password. Similarly, when you submit payment data for an online purchase, the data may contain your credit card number or other financial information. Before submitting sensitive data, look for two things that ensure the data will be submitted securely: *https* instead of http in the address, and a security icon, such as ⬛ in Internet Explorer.

Save Your Favorite Sites

If you have Web pages that you visit frequently, you can surf those pages faster by saving them as favorites within your Web browser. This enables you to display the pages with just one or two mouse clicks.

All Web browsers enable you to maintain a list of saved Web pages. In Internet Explorer, these saved sites are called *favorites*; in Firefox and Safari, saved sites are called *bookmarks*.

In each case, instead of typing an address or searching for one of these pages, you can display the Web page by selecting its address from the list of favorites or bookmarks.

Save Your Favorite Sites

SAVE A FAVORITE IN INTERNET EXPLORER

1. Display the Web page you want to save as a favorite.

2. Click the **Add to Favorites** icon (⭐).

3. Click **Add to Favorites**.

The Add a Favorite dialog box appears.

Note: *You can also display the Add a Favorite dialog box by pressing* Ctrl + D.

4. Edit the page name, as necessary.

5. Click **Add**.

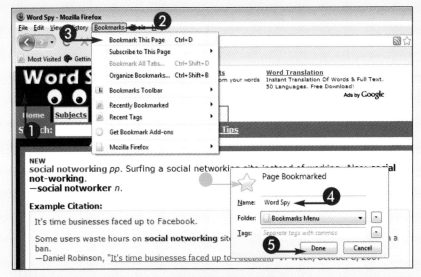

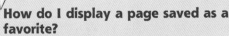

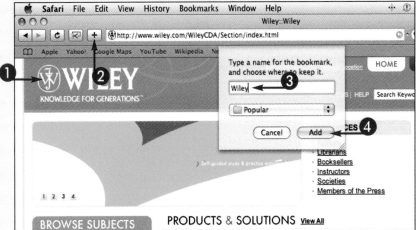

SAVE A BOOKMARK IN FIREFOX

1 Display the Web page you want to bookmark.

2 Click **Bookmarks**.

3 Click **Bookmark This Page**.

● The Page Bookmarked dialog box appears.

Note: *You can also display the Page Bookmarked dialog box by pressing* Ctrl + D.

4 Edit the page name, as necessary.

5 Click **Done**.

SAVE A BOOKMARK IN SAFARI

1 Display the Web page you want to bookmark.

2 Click the **Add Bookmark** icon (⊞).

Note: *You can also add a bookmark by pressing* ⌘ + D.

3 Edit the page name, as necessary.

4 Click **Add**.

Simplify It

How do I display a page saved as a favorite?

In Internet Explorer, click **Favorites Center** (☆) or press Alt + C to open the Favorites Center. Click **Favorites** and then click the page you want to view.

In Firefox, click **Bookmarks** and then click the page you want to display.

In Safari, click the Bookmarks Bar folder where you stored the bookmark, and then click the page.

Is there a faster way to open a favorite?

Yes. In Internet Explorer, click ☆ to open the Favorites Center and then click **Pin the Favorites Center** (📌). You can now click any favorite to open it.

In Firefox, when you open the Page Bookmarked dialog box, use the **Folder** list to choose **Bookmarks Toolbar**.

In Safari, when you add a bookmark, click ⊞ and then click **Bookmarks Bar**.

Download Files to Your Computer

If a Web site makes files available to the public, you can save one or more of those files to your computer. Saving data from the Internet to your computer is called *downloading*.

The most common types of downloads are applications, compressed file archives, and device drivers. Note that for certain types of files, the Web browser may display the content right away instead of letting you download it. This happens for files such as text documents, PDF files, and in Internet Explorer, Microsoft Office documents such as Microsoft Word files. See "Save Web Data to Your Computer" to learn how to save these types of files to your computer.

Download Files to Your Computer

1 Surf to the page that contains a link to the file you want to download.

2 Click the link.

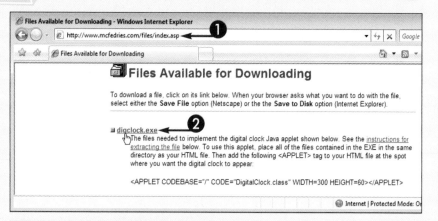

The File Download - Security Warning dialog box appears.

3 Click **Save**.

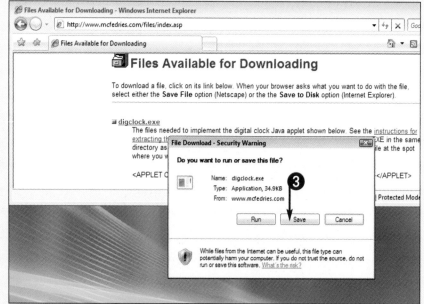

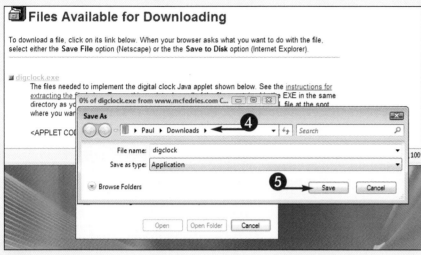

The Save As dialog box appears.

④ Choose the folder where you want to save the file.

Note: *In Windows Vista, it is best to save downloaded files to the Downloads folder associated with your user account.*

⑤ Click **Save**.

Internet Explorer downloads the file to your computer and then displays the Download Complete dialog box.

⑥ Click **Run**.

Internet Explorer opens the file.

● If you prefer to view the folder where you stored the file, click **Open Folder**, instead.

How do I download a file using Firefox or Safari?
In Firefox, click the download link and click **Save File** in the dialog box that appears. Firefox downloads the file and displays the Downloads dialog box. Double-click the file to open it; you can also right-click the file and then click **Open Containing Folder** to open the file's folder.

In Safari, click the download link. Safari downloads the file and displays it in the Downloads window. Double-click the file to open it, or click and drag the file to the folder you want.

Is it safe to download files from the Internet?
Yes, as long as you download files only from sites you trust. If your Web browser attempts to download a file without your permission, cancel the download immediately because it is likely the file contains a virus or other malware. If you do not completely trust a file you have downloaded, use an anti-virus program to scan the file before you open it.

Save Web Data to Your Computer

The Web is home to many different types of data, including pictures, videos, music, and documents. You can save a copy of a Web data file to your computer, enabling you to use the data in other documents.

If the data is in the public domain, you can use the data any way you choose. However, lots of Web data — particularly images, videos, and music — are protected by copyright. You can still copy such data, but you can use them only for personal files.

For example, if you download a copyrighted picture, your use of that image is restricted to personal documents such as greeting cards or posters, your desktop background, or other noncommercial uses.

Save Web Data to Your Computer

DOWNLOAD A PICTURE

1 Navigate to the page that contains the image you want to save.

2 Right-click the image.

3 Click Save Picture As.

Note: *In Firefox or Safari, click* **Save Image As**.

The Save Picture dialog box appears.

4 Choose the folder in which you want to save the image.

5 Type a name for the image.

6 Click **Save**.

The Web browser saves the picture to your computer.

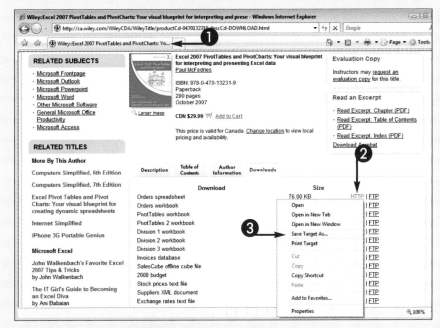

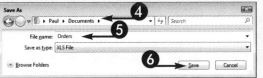

DOWNLOAD OTHER DATA

1 Navigate to the page that contains a link to the data you want to save.

2 Right-click the link.

3 Click **Save Target As**.

Note: *In Firefox, click **Save Link As**; in Safari, click **Download Linked File As**.*

The Save As dialog box appears.

4 Choose the folder in which you want to save the file.

5 Type a name for the file.

6 Click **Save**.

The Web browser saves the file to your computer.

Simplify It

How do I save the data that is currently displayed in the browser?	How do I download a file using Firefox or Safari?
In Internet Explorer, click **Page** and then click **Save As**. Choose the folder in which you want to save the data, type a name for the new file, and then click **Save**. In Firefox, click **File** and then click **Save As**. Choose the folder in which you want to save the data, type a name for the new file, and then click **Save**. In Safari, click **File** and then click **Save As**. Type a name for the new file, choose a folder, and then click **Save**.	In Firefox, click the download link and click **Save File** in the dialog box that appears. Firefox downloads the file and displays the Downloads dialog box. Double-click the file to open it; you can also right-click the file and then click **Open Containing Folder** to open the file's folder. In Safari, click the download link. Safari downloads the file and displays it in the Downloads window. Double-click the file to open it, or click and drag the file to the folder you want.

Understanding Web Error Messages

When you surf the Web, most of the time you will not encounter any problems and each site and page will appear normally. However, you may occasionally come across a site or page that does not load. In such cases, the Web server almost always returns an error code. This code usually consists of a three-digit number followed by the name of the error. In many cases you may also see an explanation of the error and steps to fix it or work around it. Note, however, that many sites implement custom error pages, so the text you see will vary from site to site.

400 Bad Request

This error means that the Web server did not understand the request for data. Most often this means that there is an error in the address. Double-check the address and try again. If the address is correct, contact the Web site and report the error.

 The webpage cannot be found

Most likely causes:
- There might be a typing error in the address.
- If you clicked on a link, it may be out of date.

401 Unauthorized Access

This error means that the Web page you are trying to display cannot be accessed without first providing authorization such as a user name and password. First make sure the address is correct. If it is, look for some kind of link to a login page. You may need to return to the site's home page to find the login link.

You are not authorized to view this page

You do not have permission to view this directory or page due to the access control list (ACL) that is configured for this resource on the Web server.

Please try the following:
- Contact the Web site administrator if you believe you should be able to view this directory or page.
- Click the Refresh button to try again with different credentials.

HTTP Error 401.3 - Unauthorized: Access is denied due to an ACL set on the requested resource.
Internet Information Services (IIS)

403 Access Forbidden

This error means that you have been denied access to the data you requested on the site. This is slightly different from the 401 Unauthorized Access error because you can get the 403 Access Forbidden error even if you have logged in to a site. The Web site has configured the data to deny access to the data. This often happens if you try to access a site directory, so try adding a file name to the address. Also, check the address for errors.

The page cannot be displayed

You have attempted to execute a CGI, ISAPI, or other executable program from a directory that does not allow programs to be executed.

Please try the following:
- Contact the Web site administrator if you believe this directory should allow execute access.

HTTP Error 403.1 - Forbidden: Execute access is denied.
Internet Information Services (IIS)

404 File Not Found

This error means that the Web server cannot find the file you requested. This is often a temporary glitch, so try reloading the page. If it still does not work, check the address to see if it contains an error. If the address is correct, the file may have been moved, so go to the site's home page and try to navigate to or search for the file from there.

> **404 Error File Not Found**
>
> The page you were requesting may no longer exist.
> Try doing a search at the top of this page or visit our homepage.

Server Error in Application "Default Web Site"

HTTP Error 500.0 - Internal Server Error

Description: This application is running in an application pool that uses the Integrated .NET mode. This is the preferred mode for running ASP.NET applications on the current and future version of IIS.

In this mode, the application using client impersonation configured with may not behave correctly. Client impersonation is not available in early ASP.NET request processing stages and may lead modules in those stages to execute with process identity instead. You have the following options:

500 Internal Server Error

This error means that the Web server encountered an internal problem when it tried to display the data you requested. This is often a temporary error, so try reloading the page or, if the error persists, try the page again later. If you still get the error, contact the Web site and report the problem.

501 Service Not Implemented

This error means that the data you requested requires a particular protocol, security system, or other service, and the Web server does not support that service. This may be a temporary error, so try reloading the page. If the error persists, try the page again later. If you keep getting the same error, report the problem to the Web site.

> **The page cannot be displayed**
>
> The page you are trying to reach cannot be retrieved.
>
> Error 501 - Not implemented

> **Error 503 - Service Unavailable**
>
> The server is temporarily unable to service your request due to maintenance downtime or capacity problems. Please try again later.
>
> *Apache/1.3.33 Server at www.notshirtnoshoesnoservice.org Port 80*

503 Service Unavailable

This error means that the Web server is not available to handle your request. The most common cause is that the Web site is too busy to handle any more requests. Try reloading the page a few times to see if you can get the data. If the error persists, it could be that the server is undergoing maintenance, so come back to the site later and try again.

Chapter 4

Surfing the Web Safely and Securely

The Web is generally a safe place to surf, shop, play, and socialize. However, all human endeavors have their share of bad apples, and the Web is no exception. Web-based threats to your computer-related security and privacy often come in the form of system intruders, stalkers, identity thieves, viruses, and spyware.

To protect yourself and your family, you need to understand these threats and to know what you can do to thwart them. This chapter introduces you to the dark side of the Web and shows you specific steps you can take to stay safe and secure online.

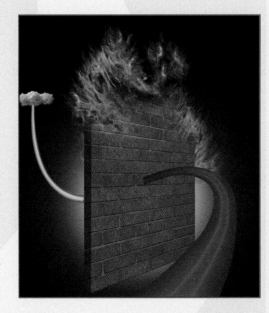

Protect Yourself on the Web

Protecting yourself on the Web means understanding and preventing a number of security and privacy problems.

These include problems with spyware, viruses, pop-up ads, saved passwords, cookies, and insecure sites.

In each case, you can take steps to guard against these threats and keep your computer and your data secure.

This section introduces you to these threats. In most cases, there are sections later in this chapter that enable you to learn more about each threat and to learn what you can do to thwart the threat.

Spyware

Spyware is a software program that installs on your computer without your knowledge or consent. This program surreptitiously gathers data from your computer, steals your passwords, displays advertisements, and takes control of your Web browser. To eliminate the program from your computer and prevent spyware from installing on your computer, you need to install an antispyware program. See "Guard Against Spyware," later in this chapter.

Viruses

A *virus* is a software program that installs on your computer surreptitiously. Some viruses are relatively benign and only display annoying messages, but most viruses are designed for nefarious purposes, such as deleting data, crashing your computer, or hijacking your computer to attack other computers. To block viruses or remove a virus from your computer, you need to install an antivirus program. See "Guard Against Viruses," later in this chapter.

Pop-up Ads

A *pop-up ad* is an advertisement that interrupts your Web browsing by appearing in a separate browser window on top of your current window. Pop-ups are annoying, but also dangerous because clicking items in the pop-up window can cause spyware or viruses to be installed on your computer. Use a pop-up blocker such as the ones built into Internet Explorer and Firefox, as described later in the "Allow Some Web Site Pop-up Windows to Appear" section.

Saved Passwords

When you submit a form that includes a site password, Internet Explorer, Firefox, and Safari display a prompt that offers to remember the password. If you click **Yes** and then access the site at a later date, the Web browser bypasses the login page and takes you directly to the site. Unfortunately, this also means that anyone else who uses your computer can access the site. Therefore, you may want to click **No** when your Web browser asks to remember the password.

Cookies

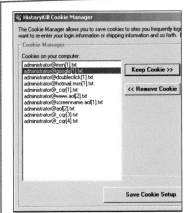

A *cookie* is a small text file that a Web site stores on your computer to keep track of things such as preferences and shopping cart items. Cookies can also store site user names and passwords, as well as your credit card data; if possible, tell the site not to save this data. Alternatively, use a cookie manager program such as HistoryKill (www.historykill.info) or Cookie Pal (www.kburra.com). See also "Delete Your Browsing History."

Insecure Sites

Secure Site Indicators

Information that you send over the Web — such as when you fill out and send a form — is usually sent in plain text that anyone can read. A secure site is one that sends your data in an encrypted format that is impossible to read. Before you send sensitive data such as your credit card number, be sure that the site is secure. In the browser address bar, look for "https" and a lock icon.

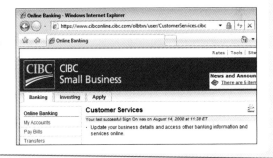

Secure Site Warnings

To help you know when you are entering a secure site, browsers such as Internet Explorer and Firefox display a warning dialog box. More importantly, these browsers also display a warning dialog box when you leave a secure site.

Protect Your Children on the Web

To protect your children on the Web means to understand the dangers that await your children and to learn ways to avoid those dangers.

It is very easy for children to come upon inappropriate material on the Web, even inadvertently. Such material includes unsuitable images, dangerous information, and inappropriate chat room conversations.

You should not underestimate the level of protection that children need. You can help protect your children by restricting the content they can view, install programs that filter out objectionable content, supervise online activities, and educate your children on the potential threats.

Potential Dangers

Unsuitable Images

The Web has no shortage of explicit or violent images that are not suitable for children. Sites that display such images usually require membership or payment, but some do not, and those sites often display unsuitable images on their home pages.

Dangerous Information

The Web is a massive storehouse of knowledge, but not all of that data is benign. There are sites where the content uses profanity, and other sites that offer inappropriate information on topics ranging from mixing chemicals to making weapons.

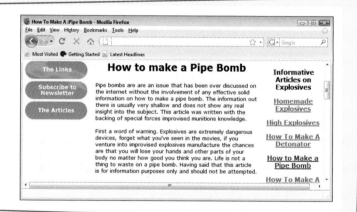

Inappropriate Chat

Adults who desire to meet young children often frequent Internet chat rooms and attempt to get young participants to reveal personal details about themselves, particularly where they live or where they go to school.

Ways to Protect Children

Restrict Content

Many Web browsers have features that restrict certain types of inappropriate Web content to authorized users. These restrictions are based on ratings that are applied to certain sites.

In Internet Explorer, select **Tools**, click **Internet Options**, and then click the **Content** tab. Use Parental Controls and the Content Advisor to restrict the actions children can perform on the Web and to control the types of content they can access.

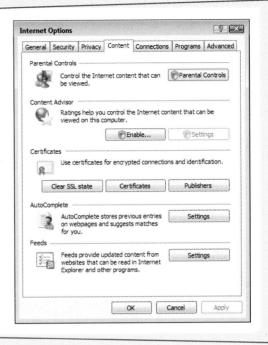

Third-Party Programs

Many third-party programs filter out content deemed objectionable to children. Among the most popular in this category are CYBERsitter (www.cybersitter.com), Net Nanny (www.netnanny.com), and CyberPatrol (www.cyberpatrol.com).

Supervision and Education

Ideally, parents should also be directly involved in protecting their children on the Web. For very young children, parents should supervise Web sessions to prevent access to inappropriate content. For older children, parents should educate them on the potential dangers and lay down ground rules for using the Web (such as not giving out personal data to strangers without permission).

Set the Web Security Level

Web pages can contain small programs, scripts, and other so-called *active* content. This active content is designed to offer you a more lively and interactive experience. However, there are ways to use such content for nefarious purposes, and some pages are set up to do just that.

Therefore, it pays to be always vigilant when you are on the Web. You can do this by setting

the appropriate security level for the Web "zone." The security level determines what types of active content can run, either with or without your permission. The higher the level, the less active content that can run, although the less interesting and interactive your Web sessions will be.

Set the Web Security Level

① Click **Start**.

② Right-click **Internet**.

③ Click **Internet Properties**.

> **Note:** If Internet Explorer is running, you can also click **Tools** and then **Internet Options**.

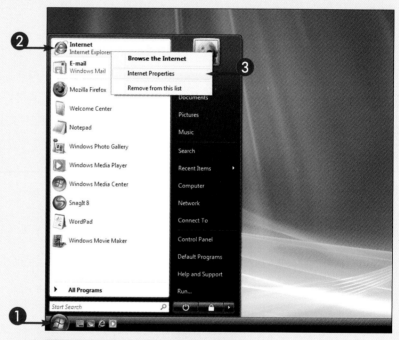

The Internet Properties dialog box appears.

④ Click the **Security** tab.

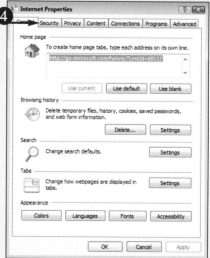

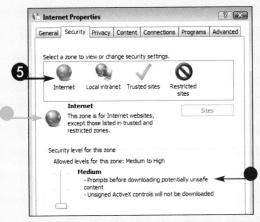

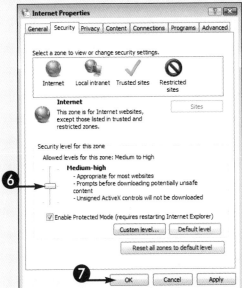

5 Click **Internet**.

● This area describes the current zone.

● This area describes the current security level for the zone.

6 Click and drag the **Security level for this zone** slider to the level you want.

*Note: If the current security level is listed as Custom, click **Default level**. This sets the security level for the Internet to Medium-high, which is a good choice for most people.*

7 Click **OK**.

Windows changes the Web security level.

Simplify It

Can I lower security for sites that I know are safe?
Yes, Internet Explorer has a "Trusted sites" zone that uses the Medium security level. This level is easier to use because you see fewer warnings and more types of content appear on the page. However, safety is also minimal, so use it only for Web sites that you trust completely. To add a site to this zone, follow steps **1** to **4**, click **Trusted sites**, click **Sites**, type the address, and click **Add**.

How can I prevent other users from downloading files?
If other people use your computer, it is often a good idea to prevent them from downloading any files from the Web. To do this, follow steps **1** to **4** and then click **Custom level** to display the Security Settings dialog box. In the Settings list, scroll down to the File download option, and then click **Disable** (◎ changes to ◉). Click **OK**.

Protect Yourself from Identity Theft

Identity theft refers to having a scammer steal data that uniquely identifies you, including your address, phone number, credit card numbers, and, most importantly, your U.S. Social Security Number (SSN) or your Canadian Social Insurance Number (SIN). The scammer uses this data to set up new credit cards, lines of credit, or loans in your name.

It can be expensive and time-consuming to straighten out such problems, and your credit rating will suffer. Therefore, it is important to take steps to ensure that you protect yourself from identity thieves while you are online.

Keep Data Private

Never give out sensitive personal data such as your SSN or SIN unless you are legally required to do so. Also, do not carry your SSN or SIN card in your wallet, just in case it gets stolen. Finally, check other cards in your wallet to ensure they do not display your SSN or SIN.

Shred Sensitive Data

Identity thieves rummage through people's garbage to look for important information such as credit card receipts and bank statements, an activity known as *dumpster diving*. To avoid sensitive data ending up in the wrong hands, purchase a high-quality shredder and shred all sensitive documents.

Check Your Credit

It is important to keep an eye on your credit history and your credit rating. Identity thieves often set up new accounts in your name, so monitoring your credit history will alert you to these new accounts. Similarly, if an identity thief racks up large debts in your name, your credit rating could plunge, so monitor your rating to look for sudden drops. Use a credit reporting agency such as Equifax (www.equifax.com) or Experian (www.experian.com).

Watch Your Mail

Incoming mail often contains useful data for an identity thief such as credit card or bank statements, new checks or credit cards, or a credit report. If possible, install a mail slot on your front door so that all mail goes inside your house. Otherwise, pick up received mail as soon as possible, or use a locked mailbox. If you have curbside mail pickup, do not use it to mail checks or other sensitive data. Suspend mail delivery when you go on vacation.

Stop Prescreened Offers

Credit card and insurance companies often send out credit or insurance offers to customers that have been preapproved (or prescreened). Unfortunately, these offers often contain sensitive data useful to an identity thief. Use a service such as OptOutPrescreen.com to opt out of such offers.

Guard Against Phishing

Phishing

Phishing refers to creating a replica of an existing Web page to fool a user into submitting personal, financial, or password data. The most common ploy is to copy the Web page code from a major site — such as AOL or eBay — and use it to set up a replica page that appears to be part of the company's site. Phishers send out a fake e-mail with a link to this page, which solicits the user's credit card data or password. When a recipient submits the form, it sends the data to the scammer.

Detect Phishing

Learn the tell-tale signs of a phishing attempt. First, examine the addresses associated with e-mail or Web page links, and look for addresses that point to pages on the phisher's site. A legitimate page will have the correct domain — such as aol.com or ebay.com — whereas a phishing page will have only something similar — such as *aol.whatever.com* or *blah.com/ebay*. Look for text or images that are not associated with the trustworthy site. Finally, look for secure site indicators such as https in the address and a lock icon.

Turn on Phishing Filter

Internet Explorer comes with a phishing filter that can block known phishing sites and warn you about potential phishing scams. Click **Tools**, click **Phishing Filter**, and then click **Turn On Automatic Website Checking**. If you see **Suspicious Website** in the address bar, do not interact with the site.

Guard Against Spyware

Spyware is a software program that surreptitiously gathers data from your computer, steals your passwords, displays advertisements, or hijacks your Web browser. In most cases, the program installs itself on your computer without your direct knowledge or consent.

Because spyware is often difficult or even impossible to remove from your computer, you should take steps to prevent it from ever installing on your machine. This means understanding how spyware gets installed, and knowing the best ways to avoid infection. If you use Windows Vista, you should also ensure that its antispyware program, Windows Defender, is configured to thwart spyware.

Spyware Installation

There are many different ways that spyware can install itself on your computer. The most common method is when the spyware comes bundled with another program, such as a screen saver, download utility, or even an alleged antispyware program. Another common source is a pop-up window that claims you must install a program to view the site or repair your computer.

Be Wary

Although some spyware can install itself without your knowledge, most spyware requires your participation, usually in the form of clicking a button on a Web page or in a pop-up window. A site will attempt to entice you to click the button by claiming your computer has system errors, or by offering an excellent and short-lived deal. Be wary of such lies, and always remember that if something appears to be too good to be true, it almost always is.

Check Programs

It is not dangerous to download software from major sites, but smaller distributors and sites can be quite dangerous because their downloads often come with a spyware payload. Many programs are known spyware carriers, so check out a program before installing it. Use a site such as www.spywareguide.com.

Closing Pop-ups

If you come across a pop-up window that is suspicious, you should close the window to avoid infection. However, you need to exercise some caution here. The pop-up might show a button named "Close" or "Cancel," but it could be a decoy that only starts the installation. The only safe way to close a pop-up is to press `Ctrl` + `W` (or `⌘` + `W` on a Mac). If the window does not close, shut down your other applications and restart your computer.

Guard Against Spyware

① Click **Start**.

② Click **All Programs**.

③ Click **Windows Defender**.

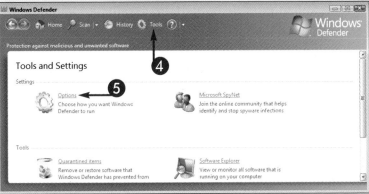

The Windows Defender antispyware program appears.

④ Click **Tools**.

⑤ Click **Options.**

⑥ Click **Automatically scan my computer** (☐ changes to ☑).

⑦ Click **Use real-time protection** (☐ changes to ☑).

⑧ Click **Save**.

The User Account Control dialog box appears.

⑨ Enter your User Account Control credentials.

Your computer is now protected against spyware.

Guard Against Viruses

A *virus* is a malicious software program that installs on your computer surreptitiously. Some viruses only display annoying messages, but most are designed to either damage your system by deleting data or crashing your computer, or to hijack your computer and use it to attack other computers.

You can reduce the danger of accidentally unleashing a virus on your computer by taking care with e-mail attachments and by reading all your e-mail messages in text format.

It is also very important to note that neither Windows nor Mac OS X come with an antivirus program. Therefore, one of the first things you should do with any new computer is purchase and install a good antivirus program.

Take Care with Attachments

Never open an attachment that comes from someone you do not know. Even if you know the sender, if the attachment is not something you are expecting, there is a good chance that the sender's system is infected. Examine the message text to see if it makes sense in the context of your relationship with that person, and is not just some generic message such as "Check this out!" (or something similar). If you are not sure, write back and confirm that the sender e-mailed the message.

Do Not Open Executable Files

When dealing with a Web page link or an e-mail attachment, examine the file name. If the link or message text says the file is a picture and the file name ends with a graphics extension (such as .jpg or .gif), then it is probably okay; if the file name ends with an executable extension (such as .exe, .bat, or .vbs), then definitely do not open it. Note that Outlook and Windows Mail automatically block potentially dangerous executable attachments.

Antivirus Software

Be sure to install a top-of-the-line antivirus program, particularly one that checks incoming e-mail. In addition, be sure to keep your antivirus program's virus list up-to-date. As you read this, there are probably dozens, maybe even hundreds, of malicious hackers designing even nastier viruses. Regular updates will help you keep up. Some security suites to check out are Norton Internet Security (www.symantec.com), McAfee Internet Security Suite (www.mcafee.com), and Avast! Antivirus (www.avast.com).

Scan Downloaded Files

Files that come from reputable Web sites are almost certainly virus-free. However, if you download a file from a site you do not know or do not trust, you should use your antivirus software to scan the file for infection before opening it. This also applies to e-mail attachments that you are not sure about. Save the attachment to your hard drive and then scan it.

Guard Against Viruses

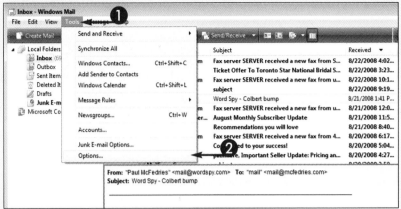

① In Windows Mail or Outlook Express, click **Tools**.

② Click **Options**.

The Options dialog box appears.

③ Click the **Read** tab.

④ Click **Read all messages in plain text** (☐ changes to ☑).

⑤ Click **OK**.

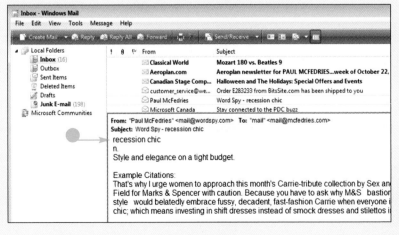

● E-mail messages now appear only in plain text.

Note: *When you are viewing a message as plain text, you may realize that the message is innocuous and that it is okay to view the HTML version. To switch quickly to HTML, click* ***View*** *and then click* ***Message in HTML***. *You can also press* Alt + Shift + H.

Delete Your Browsing History

To ensure that other people who have access to your computer cannot view information from sites you have visited, you can delete your browsing history.

As you visit Web sites, Internet Explorer maintains information about the sites you visit. Internet Explorer also maintains a folder called Temporary Internet Files which stores copies of page text, images, and other content so that

sites load faster the next time you view them. Similarly, Internet Explorer also saves text and passwords that you have typed into forms.

Saving all this data is useful because it enables you to quickly revisit a site. However, it is also dangerous because other people who use your computer can just as easily visit or view information about those sites.

Delete Your Browsing History

1. Click **Tools**.

2. Click **Delete Browsing History**.

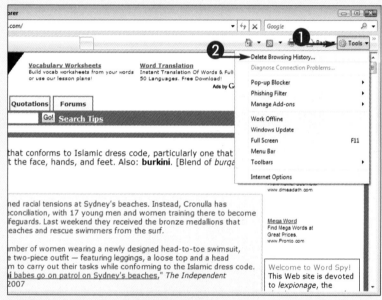

The Delete Browsing History dialog box appears.

3. To delete a specific part of your browsing history, click the appropriate button.

Internet Explorer asks you to confirm.

4. Click **Yes**.

Internet Explorer deletes the specified browsing history.

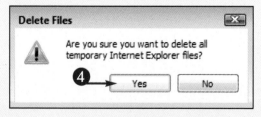

⑤ Repeat steps **3** and **4** to delete other parts of your browsing history.

⑥ To delete all of your browsing history, click **Delete all**.

Internet Explorer asks you to confirm.

⑦ Click **Yes**.

Internet Explorer deletes all the browsing history and closes the Delete Browsing History dialog box.

If you did not delete all your browsing history, click **Close** to shut down the Delete Browsing History dialog box.

Simplify It

How do I delete browsing history in Firefox?
Follow these steps:

❶ Click **Tools**.

❷ Click **Clear Private Data**.

❸ Select the check box beside each type of data you want to delete (☐ changes to ☑).

❹ Click **Clear Private Data Now**.

Firefox removes the selected browsing history.

How do I delete browsing history in Safari?
Follow these steps:

❶ Click **Safari** (Mac OS X) or **Edit** (Windows).

❷ Click **Reset Safari**.

❸ Select the check box beside each type of data you want to delete (☐ changes to ☑).

❹ Click **Reset**.

Safari removes the selected browsing history.

Allow Some Web Site Pop-up Windows to Appear

You can improve your surfing experience by configuring Internet Explorer to view the pop-up ads for certain Web sites that Internet Explorer would otherwise block.

Web page advertising is necessary because sites often need money from advertisers to help defray the costs of maintaining a site. To make more of an impact, advertisers often insist that their ads appear in separate pop-up windows. Unfortunately, these pop-up ads can make surfing the Web more annoying and more time-consuming, so Internet Explorer blocks all pop-up windows.

However, some sites display useful information such as a media player or a login message in pop-up windows, and Internet Explorer may block these windows. If so, you can add the site's address to the list of sites that are allowed to display pop-ups.

Allow Some Web Site Pop-up Windows to Appear

❶ Click **Tools**.

❷ Click **Pop-up Blocker**.

❸ Click **Pop-up Blocker Settings**.

The Pop-up Blocker Settings dialog box appears.

❹ Type that site address in the **Address of website to allow** text box.

❺ Click **Add**.

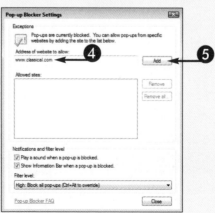

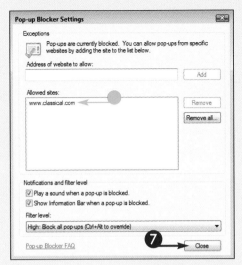

- Internet Explorer includes the address in the **Allowed sites** list.

⑥ Repeat steps **4** and **5** to add other sites to the Allowed sites list.

⑦ Click **Close**.

⑧ Restart Internet Explorer.

The next time you visit the site, Internet Explorer displays its pop-up windows.

Simplify It

Is there a faster way to allow a site's pop-ups?
Yes, instead of typing a site's address in the Pop-up Blocker Settings dialog box, an easier method is to navigate to the site and look for the Internet Explorer Information Bar that appears when the program blocks a pop-up. Click the Information Bar, click **Always Allow Pop-ups from This Site**, and then click **Yes** when Internet Explorer asks you to confirm.

How do I allow a site's pop-ups in Firefox or Safari?
In Firefox, click **Tools** and then click **Options** to open the Options dialog box. Click the **Content** tab. Click the **Exceptions** button beside the **Block pop-up windows** check box to open the Allowed Sites - Pop-ups dialog box. Type the site address, click **Allow**, and then click **Close**.

Unfortunately, Safari does not offer an option for allowing a site's pop-ups.

Create a Strong Password

Many Web sites require a password to access the site's content. For example, on many sites you must log in to access restricted content that is available only to registered users or paid subscribers. On e-commerce sites, you often have an account that is password-protected so that you can place orders and track shipments. Finally, a password is a must for secure sites such as online banking and corporate pages.

Each of these scenarios has a different level of security, but in each case you do not want an unauthorized person to log in using your account. The best way to prevent unauthorized access is to protect your account with a strong password.

Password Length

Be sure to use a password that is at least eight characters long. Shorter passwords are susceptible to programs that try every letter combination. You can combine the 26 letters of the alphabet into about 12 million different five-letter word combinations, which is no big deal for a fast program. If you bump things up to eight-letter passwords, however, the total number of combinations rises to 200 billion, which would take even the fastest computer quite a while.

Password Complexity

Add complexity to your password by mixing up your character types. The secret to a strong password is to include characters from the following categories: lowercase letters, uppercase letters, numbers, and symbols. If you include at least one character from three (or, even better, all four) of these categories, you are well on your way to a strong password.

Password Checking

How will you know whether the password you've come up with fits the definition of *strong*? One way to find out is to submit the password to an online password complexity checker, such as the Microsoft Password Checker available at www.microsoft.com/protect/yourself/password/checker.mspx. Type your password in the Password box and make sure the Strength indicator says either Strong or Best.

Security At Home > Personal Information

Password checker

Your online accounts, computer files, and personal information are more secure when you use strong passwords to help protect them.

Test the strength of your passwords: Enter a password in the text box to have Password Checker help determine its strength as you type.

Password: ●●●●●●●●●●●●●

Strength: | | | Strong |

Note: Password Checker can help you to gauge the strength of your password. It is for personal reference only. Password Checker does not guarantee the security of the password itself.

Remove Saved Passwords

If you have used your Web browser to save passwords, you might prefer to remove some or all of those passwords for security.

Internet Explorer

With Internet Explorer, you can only delete all saved passwords. Click **Tools** and then click **Delete Browsing History**. In the Delete Browsing History dialog box, click **Delete passwords** and then click **Yes** when Internet Explorer asks you to confirm. Click **Close**.

Firefox

With Firefox, you can remove some or all of your saved passwords. Click **Tools** and then click **Options**. In the Options dialog box, click the **Security** tab and then click **Saved Passwords**. In the Saved Passwords dialog box, click the password you want to delete and then click **Remove**. To delete all saved passwords, instead, click **Remove All** and then click **Yes**. When you are done, click **Close**.

Safari

With Safari, you can remove some or all of your saved passwords. Click **Safari** (in OS X) or **Edit** (in Windows) and then click **Preferences**. Click the **AutoFill** tab and then click **Edit** beside the **User names and passwords** check box. Click the password you want to delete and then click **Remove**. To delete all saved passwords, instead, click **Remove All**. When you are finished, click **Done**.

Chapter 5

Searching for Information on the Web

The Web is home to billions of Web pages, so how do you know which page to visit? It often helps to ask friends and family to recommend a site. However, if you need information on a specific topic, there are free Web sites called *search engines* that enable you to quickly search the Web for pages that have the information you require.

You can search the Web either by going directly to a search engine site or by using the search feature built into your browser.

Understanding Search Engines

The Web now holds so many pages that it is impossible for any one person to know even a small fraction of what is available. Word of mouth, newspaper articles, magazine stories, and even other Web pages are great ways to learn what pages are out there.

However, to find quality information that is relevant to whatever you are interested in, you need a tool to help you. On the Web, that tool is a search engine. This section introduces you to search engines so you can get more out of the sections that follow and choose the search engine that is right for your needs.

Search Engine

A *search engine* is a special Web site that has stored much of the content on the Web in a giant database. This database is *indexed*, which means that the search engine tracks keywords and other terms in each page. When you enter a search term into the search engine, it returns a list of the pages that match your term.

Web Crawler

Search engines index the Web by using special programs called *Web crawlers* — also called spiders or robots — to catalog each Web page and its content. Most search engines also enable individuals to submit information about their Web pages. Google, the largest search engine, indexes hundreds of billions of Web pages with its Googlebot crawler.

Search Engine Sites

Here are the addresses of some popular search engines:

Google	www.google.com
Yahoo!	www.yahoo.com
Live Search	www.live.com
Ask	www.ask.com
AltaVista	www.altavista.com
My Web Search	www.mywebsearch.com

Search Types

By default, search engines return links to those Web pages that match your search criteria. However, the Web is about more than just text. It also contains images, music and audio files, video files, news, and more. Most of the larger search engines enable you to search for these different types of content.

Subject Directory

The Web is so large that many search engines have Web site directories that list sites by subject (such as Arts, Business, or Science). To ensure the quality of the information contained on each site, employees of the search engine usually review the sites listed in these subject directories.

Advanced Searches

Be default, the search engine looks for pages that contain the search term you enter. If you enter multiple terms, the search engine matches sites that contain all the terms. If you want to match an exact phrase, or just one of several terms, then you need to use the search engine's advanced search feature, which is offered by most major search engines.

Site Searching

Do not confuse searching the Web as a whole with searching just a particular site. Many Web sites come with a search feature, but it usually applies only to content on the site itself. That is, you enter a search term and the site returns a list of pages from that site that match your term.

Search from the Web Browser

If you need information on a specific topic, your Web browser has a built-in feature that enables you to quickly search the Web for sites that have the information you require. That is, you can enter the search term within the browser itself, instead of first surfing to the search engine site.

Note that a search engine still performs the search. For example, Internet Explorer uses the Live Search service when you search the Web from that browser. Both Firefox and Safari use Google as their default search engines. Internet Explorer and Firefox also enable you to customize the search engine to use the one that you prefer.

Search from the Web Browser

SEARCH USING INTERNET EXPLORER

① Click in the **Instant Search** box.

② Type a word, phrase, or question that represents the information you want to find.

③ Click the **Search** button (🔎).

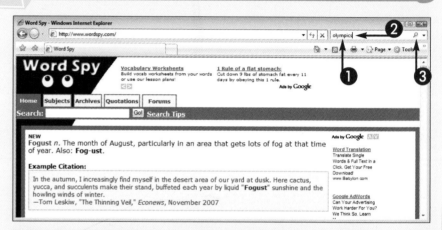

● A list of pages that match your search text appears.

④ Click a Web page.

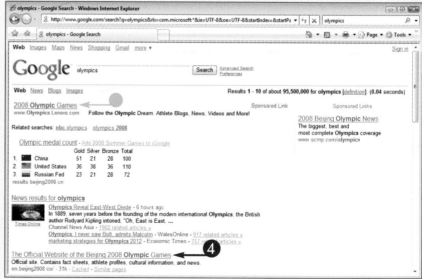

SEARCH USING FIREFOX

1 Click in the **Search** box.

2 Type a word, phrase, or question that represents the information you want to find.

3 Click the **Search** button (🔍).

A list of pages that match your search text appears.

SEARCH USING SAFARI

1 Click in the **Search** box.

2 Type a word, phrase, or question that represents the information you want to find.

3 Press Return.

A list of pages that match your search text appears.

Simplify It

Can I use another search engine in Internet Explorer?
Yes. To add another search engine, click the search box ▾ and then click **Find More Providers**. Click the search engine you want to use and then click **Add Provider**. To use the search engine, click the search box ▾ and then click the search engine name.

Can I use another search engine in Firefox?
Yes. Click the search box ▾. If you do not see the search engine you want, click **Manage Search Engines** and then click **Get more search engines**. In the Web page that appears, locate your search engine, click the engine's **Add to Firefox** link, and then click **Add**. To use the search engine, click the search box ▾ and then click the search engine name.

Search Using Google

Google is by far the most popular search engine, and most people believe it returns the most relevant results, so you should know how this important Web tool works.

The Google search engine began as a research project conducted by two graduate students at Stanford University in the mid-1990s. The project discovered that the number of pages that link to a given site is an excellent indicator of the popularity and quality of the site, so this information formed the backbone of the new search engine. Google now indexes over one trillion Web pages.

Search Using Google

1 Click inside the address bar of your Web browser.

2 Delete the existing address.

3 Type **http://www.google.com/**.

4 Press Enter or Return.

The Google home page appears.

5 Type a word, phrase, or question that represents the information you want to find.

6 Click **Google Search**.

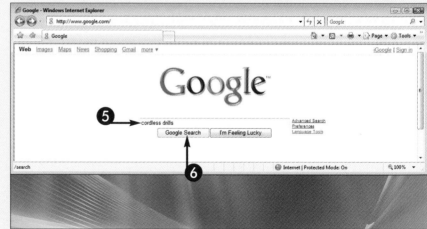

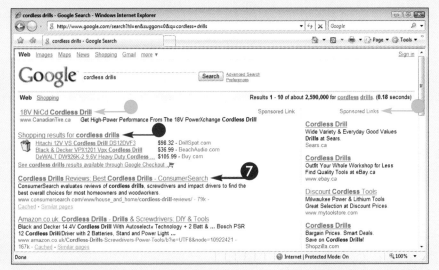

● Results that appear in the Sponsored Links sections have been paid for by advertisers.

● A list of pages that match your search text appears.

⑦ Click a link to a Web page.

Note: Choose the Web page that appears to most closely match the information you seek.

The page appears.

*Note: If this page does not contain the information you are looking for, click your browser's **Back** button to return to the Google search results and then click a different link.*

Can I use Google to search for data other than Web pages?
Yes, the Google search engine can locate images, news articles, newsgroup posts, blog posts, and more. At the top of the Google home page, click the link for the type of data you want to search: **Images**, **Maps**, **News**, or **Shopping**. You can also click **more** to see more search types, including **Video**, **Groups**, **Books**, and **Blogs**.

What does the I'm Feeling Lucky button do?
After you type your search text, if you click **I'm Feeling Lucky** instead of Google Search, Google automatically sends you to the site that best matches your search text. (That is, the site that appears at the top of the search results.) If you are fairly confident that the top-ranking search result will be the site you want, use I'm Feeling Lucky to save yourself a bit of time.

Refine Your Google Searches

You can refine your Google searches to get much more specific results. This is particularly useful if you do not find a good match when you try a standard Google search.

By default, Google looks for pages that match all of the words you specify, in any order. However, you can refine your search to return sites that match an exact phrase, that match one or more of your words, or that do not contain a particular word.

You can also refine your Google search by restricting it to a specific Web site, either by date or by specifying a numeric range (for example if you are price shopping).

Refine Your Google Searches

① Navigate to the Google home page.

② Click **Advanced Search**.

> *Note: The Advanced Search link is also available in the results page of any Google Web search.*

The Advanced Search page appears.

③ Type the words that must appear in the matching pages.

④ Type an exact phrase that must appear in the matching pages.

⑤ Type up to three words or phrases if you want the matching pages to include one or more of these words or phrases.

⑥ Type the words that must not appear in the matching pages.

⑦ Type the site you want to search.

⑧ Click this link.

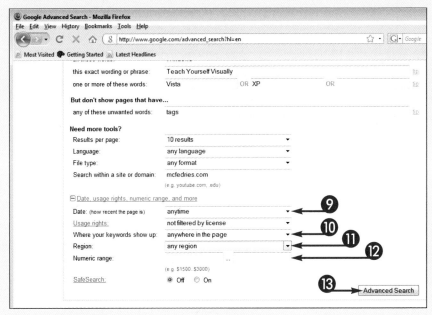

Google shows more search options.

9 Click ⊡ and then click a date.

10 Click ⊡ and then click where you want Google to look for your search terms.

11 Click ⊡ and choose the country you want to search.

12 Use these text boxes to enter a numeric range.

13 Click **Advanced Search**.

Google displays the search results.

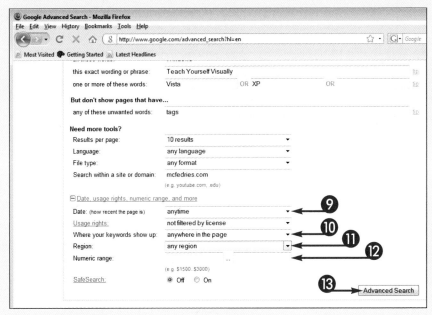

Simplify It

Do I have to use the Advanced Search form to refine my Google searches?
No, you can use special words and characters — called *operators* — in the regular search box:

""	Surround words with quotation marks to search for the exact phrase ("espresso machine")
OR	Use this operator (you must use uppercase letters) to match one word or another (espresso OR cappuccino)
-	Place this operator in front of a word to match pages that do not include the word (espresso -expresso)
site:	Use this operator to search within a site (site:coffeegeek.com)
..	Use this operator to enter a numeric range ("espresso machine" $1000..$2000)

Get More Out of Google Searching

Google offers a number of options — called *preferences* — that you can use to configure your search results and get more out of Google.

For example, you can configure Google to only return results written in one or more languages. By default, Google returns results from all languages, but you might want to restrict the results to a particular language, such as English.

You can also configure Google's SafeSearch feature, which blocks pages that contain explicit text or images.

Finally, you can also configure the number of results Google displays on each page. The default is 10, but you can configure Google to display up to 100 pages at once in the results.

① Navigate to the Google home page.

② Click **Preferences**.

Note: *The Preferences link is also available in the results page of any Google Web search.*

The Preferences page appears.

③ Click **Prefer pages written in these language(s)** (◎ changes to ⦿).

④ Click the check box beside the language you want to use (☐ changes to ☑).

Note: *Repeat step 4 to specify as many languages as you want to use.*

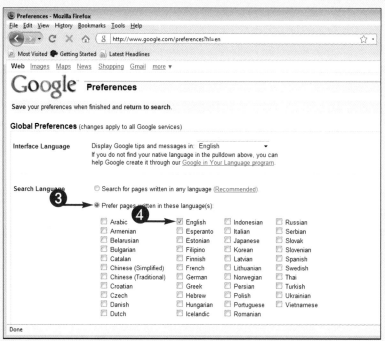

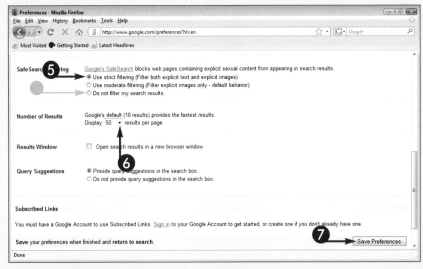

⑤ If you do not want to see explicit text or images in your search results, click **Use strict filtering** (◎ changes to ◉).

● If you prefer that Google not block any pages, click **Do not filter my search results**, instead (◎ changes to ◉).

⑥ Click ⊡, and then click the number of pages you want to see in the results.

⑦ Click **Save Preferences**.

⑧ Click **OK**.

Google returns you to the Google home page.

Simplify It

Is there a way to turn off the suggestions that Google displays as I type my search terms?
Yes. The search suggestions are occasionally helpful, but they are mostly distracting. To turn them off, follow steps **1** and **2** to open the Preferences page. Scroll down to the **Query Suggestions** section and click the **Do not provide query suggestions in the search box** option (◎ changes to ◉). Click **Save Preferences** and then click **OK**.

Is there a way to search for pages from a certain country?
Yes. On the Google home page, click **Language Tools** to open the Language Tools page. Scroll down to the **Visit Google's Site in Your Local Domain** section and then click the country you want to search. Click the **pages from** *Country* option (◎ changes to ◉), where *Country* is the name of the country you chose. Run your search and Google returns pages just from that country.

Search for Information Using Wikipedia

Wikipedia is a free online encyclopedia that is one of the Web's largest reference sites, so you should know how to use it to do research.

The unique feature of Wikipedia is that it is not written by professionals. Instead, it is a collaborative Web site that allows any registered user to add, edit, and delete the site's content. Wikipedia currently has more than 75,000 contributors, and collectively they have created more than 2.5 million articles in English — and more than 10 million articles in all languages.

Although you can browse Wikipedia, the site is so large that it is usually faster and easier to search for the information you want.

Search for Information Using Wikipedia

① Click inside the address bar of your Web browser.

② Delete the existing address.

③ Type **http://en.wikipedia. org/**.

④ Press **Enter** or **Return**.

Note: *If you want to view Wikipedia in a language other than English, go to wikipedia.org and then click the language you want.*

The Wikipedia main page appears.

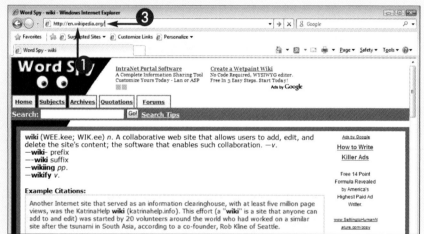

⑤ Use the **search** box to type a word or phrase that represents the information you want to find.

⑥ Click **Go**.

● If you want to search all of the Wikipedia content (and not just article titles), click **Search**, instead.

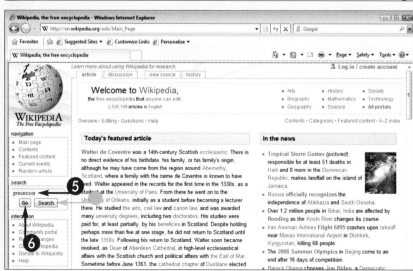

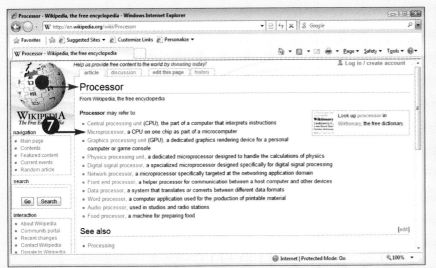

● A list of articles that match your search text appears.

Note: If you typed the exact title of an article in step 5, Wikipedia displays the article.

⑦ Click the link that represents the article you want.

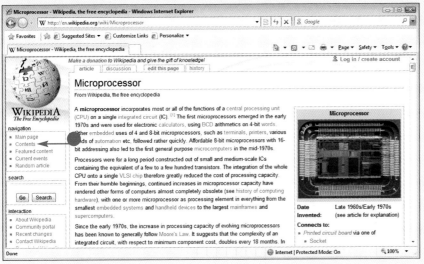

The article appears.

● If you prefer to browse the Wikipedia articles, click **Contents** and then use the links to browse articles alphabetically or by category.

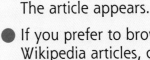

Are the Wikipedia articles accurate and complete?
Wikipedia has tens of thousands of highly knowledgeable volunteers, many of whom spend hours each day checking articles for errors, sources, and vandalism. Therefore, most of the articles on Wikipedia are accurate and reasonably complete. However, because anyone can edit articles, some errors are inevitable, so you should always double-check Wikipedia information with other sources.

Can I edit Wikipedia articles?
Yes, anyone can edit almost any Wikipedia article. However, you can only do so if you are registered with the site. In any Wikipedia page, click the **Log in / create account** link, click the **Create one** link, and then provide a user name, password, and optional e-mail address.

Discover Other Search Engines

Search engines such as Google and Yahoo! index as much of the Web as their crawlers can access, which makes them good choices for general searches. However, if you are looking for information in a specific topic area, you might be better off using a search engine that specializes in that topic.

These are often called *specialty search engines*, and they are better for topic-specific searches because they usually return more relevant results than a general search engine. Even more important, specialty search engines are often built upon databases that the general search engines cannot access, so specialty search engines usually return higher information.

Internet Movie Database

The Internet Movie Database (www.imdb.com) is a massive collection of information on nearly 400,000 movies. For each film you get the names (and links to) the actors, director, and writers, plot summaries, stats (such as the film's running time), trivia, user reviews, and much more. See also CinemaReview.com.

Technorati

Use Technorati Search (search.technorati.com) to locate information in more than 100 million blogs. You can also use the main Technorati site (technorati.com) to browse blogs in various categories, including Technology, Sports, and Entertainment.

Scirus

Scirus (www.scirus.com) is a science search engine. You can use it to search for scientific information not only in online journals, but also in the Web pages of scientists, online course materials, and more. In all, Scirus indexes over 450 million science-related items.

AardvarkSport

If you need to search for sports-related information, check out AardvarkSport (www.aardvarksport.net), which boasts a large database of sport sites from all around the world.

PriceGrabber

PriceGrabber (www.pricegrabber.com) is one of the Web's most popular shopping search engines (also called a *shopping portal*). When you search for a product, PriceGrabber's results provide you with lots of information: price, stock, product details, user reviews and discussions, expert reviews, seller rating, and taxes and shipping for your zip code. See also ShopZilla.com.

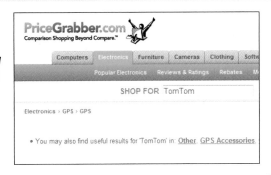

All Recipes

All Recipes (www.allrecipes.com) is home to thousands of recipes for any type of food and any type of cuisine. For each recipe, you get a picture, an ingredients list, cooking instructions, cooking times, nutritional information, and user reviews.

Whois.net

If you have ever wondered who owns a particular domain name, you can use Whois.net (www.whois.net) to find out. When you perform a WHOIS Lookup, Whois.net returns the name and address of the company or person who owns the domain.

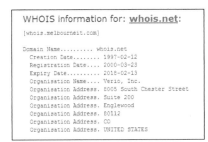

Search Engine Guide

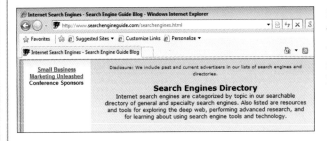

There are hundreds of specialty search engines on the Web, so this section has only grazed the surface of what is available. For a more complete list, see Search Engine Guide Blog's Search Engines Directory (www.searchengineguide.com/searchengines.html).

Search a Web Page

If a Web page contains information you need, you may have to search the page to locate the information.

When a Web page contains only a small amount of text, it is usually easy to find the information you want on that page just by scanning the text. However, many Web pages contain hundreds or even thousands of words, so scanning the text to find what you want can be time-consuming. A much faster method is to use your Web browser's built-in Find feature to search for a word or phrase associated with the information you need.

Search a Web Page

SEARCH A PAGE WITH INTERNET EXPLORER 8

① Press **Ctrl** + **F**.

● The Find bar appears.

② Type your search text.

● Internet Explorer highlights the first match.

● Internet Explorer displays the total number of matches.

③ Click **Next** to find more matches.

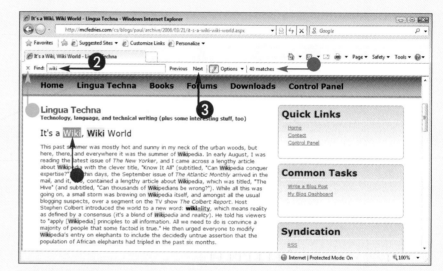

SEARCH A PAGE WITH INTERNET EXPLORER 7

① Press **Ctrl** + **F**.

● The Find dialog box appears.

② Type your search text.

③ Click **Next**.

● Internet Explorer highlights the first match.

④ Click **Next** to find more matches.

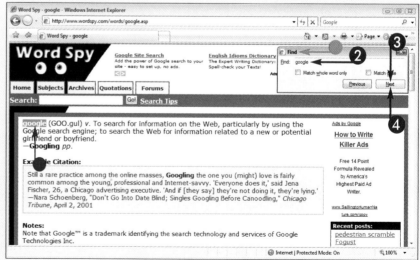

SEARCH A PAGE WITH FIREFOX

❶ Press `Ctrl` + `F`.

● The Find Bar appears.

❷ Type your search text.

● Firefox highlights the first match.

❸ Click **Next** to find more matches.

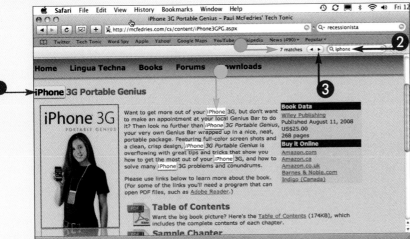

SEARCH A PAGE WITH SAFARI

❶ Press `⌘` + `F`.

● The Find banner appears.

❷ Type your search text.

● Safari highlights the first match in yellow.

● Safari highlights the total other matches in white.

❸ Click the **Next** arrow to find more matches.

Simplify It

How do I search for a word that uses a specific combination of uppercase and lowercase letters?
With Internet Explorer 8, click **Options** in the Find Bar and then click **Match Case**. With Internet Explorer 7, click the **Match Case** check box (☐ changes to ☑) in the Find dialog box. In Firefox, click the **Match case** check box (☐ changes to ☑) in the Find Bar. Safari does not support case-sensitive searches.

How do I search for entire words instead of partial words?
With Internet Explorer 8, click **Options** in the Find Bar and then click **Match Whole Word Only**. With Internet Explorer 7, click the **Match whole word only** check box (☐ changes to ☑) in the Find dialog box. Neither Firefox nor Safari support whole-word searches.

Chapter 6

Getting Things Done on the Web

The sheer wealth of data on the World Wide Web means that, no matter what your age, tastes, or interests, there is no shortage of things to do while you are online. You can keep informed by reading news and doing research; you can socialize with others and play games; you can do your banking and investing, and then use that money to book your dream vacation online; you can find a job, keep your kids occupied, and even create your own Web site. This chapter gives you lots of information about all of these Web pastimes.

Read News on the Web

The Web is a perfect venue for reading news because you get a wide range of stories from a variety of viewpoints. And since Web pages are so quickly and easily updated, online news stories are usually timely and up-to-the-minute.

For all these reasons, the Web is home to many sites that enable you to read the latest news.

For example, many newspapers, magazines, and other print sources have Web sites. There are also many magazines that exist only online, and there are more recent innovations such as Web logs.

TV Network News

All major television networks with large news divisions have Web sites that complement their traditional content, particularly with videos and photos. These sites include CNN (cnn.com), Fox (www.foxnews.com), ABC (abcnews.go.com), CBS (www.cbsnews.com), MSNBC (www.msnbc.msn.com), CBC in Canada (www.cbcnews.ca), and the BBC in Britain (news.bbc.co.uk).

Newspapers and Magazines

Print media such as newspapers and magazines have embraced the Web as a way to augment their traditional business. Some companies have Web sites with up-to-the-minute stories, whereas others use their sites just as archives of previously published stories. Some media sites require that you register in order to access the articles, but on most sites, the registration is free.

Online Magazines

A number of Web news sources exist only as online magazines, also called *e-zines*. The best of these online publications offer a wide variety of content and excellent writing. Some of the best are Salon (www.salon.com), Slate (www.slate.com), and Flak (www.flakmag.com).

Web Logs

A *Web log*, or *blog*, is a Web page consisting of frequently updated, reverse-chronological entries on a particular topic. Some blogs are mere diaries or lists of interesting links, but many have a news focus, particularly news on politics — such as Instapundit.com — and technology — such as TechCrunch (www.techcrunch.com). See Chapter 13 to learn much more about reading blogs and even creating your own blog.

User-Driven News

A *user-driven* news site is one where users suggest or nominate news stories and other users vote on whether those stories are interesting or relevant. The stories that get the most votes end up on the "front page" of the site. User-driven news sites include Digg (www.digg.com), Reddit (www.reddit.com), and Propeller (www.propeller.com).

News Portal

A *news portal* is a Web site that gathers news from hundreds or even thousands of online sources. You can then search the news, browse headlines, and view news by subject. Two popular news portals are NewsIsFree (www.newsisfree.com) and NewsNow (www. newsnow.co.uk). The major search engines also maintain news portals, such as Google News (news.google.com) and Yahoo! News (news.yahoo.com).

News Syndication

Instead of surfing to a Web media site or news portal, you can have articles and news headlines sent to you. Many news sites use *syndication*, which enables a special program called an aggregator — also called an RSS reader (RSS is short for Really Simple Syndication) — to display the syndicated content. Firefox and the latest versions of Internet Explorer and Safari have aggregators built in. You can also use online tools such as Newsgator (www.newsgator.com) and Google Reader (www.google.com/reader).

Research Using the Web

You can use the Web's vast resources to research just about any topic you can think of. The Web has information that can help you with a school project, your family history, or a presentation at work. You can search for the data that you need, or go to specific research sites.

However, be aware that not all the information on the Web is factual or useful. Sites often have inaccurate or deliberately misleading data. In general, stick to large, reputable sites. If you are not sure, ask your friends, family, or colleagues to recommend sites they use.

Reference Materials

Sites such as Encarta (encarta.msn.com) and Britannica (www.britannica.com) offer multiple online research tools, including encyclopedias, dictionaries, and atlases. Remember, too, that Wikipedia has millions of user-created articles, as described in Chapter 5. The Web is also home to thousands of sites that offer almanacs, maps, and thesauruses.

Libraries

Many public and private libraries maintain Web sites that enable you to search their catalogs, access their digital archives, and even order books if you live nearby and have a library card or account. Examples include the New York Public Library (www.nypl.org) and the Library of Congress (www.loc.gov). There are also online libraries, such as the Internet Public Library (www.ipl.org), that catalog Internet sites.

Museums

There are thousands of museums online covering every imaginable topic, from art to history to science. Most sites offer a list of current and upcoming exhibits, articles, and education resources. Examples include the Smithsonian Institution (www.si.edu), the American Museum of Natural History (www.amnh.org), and the British Museum (www.britishmuseum.org). For a useful database of museum Web sites, see Museum Stuff (www.museumstuff.com).

Government Resources

Federal, state, and municipal government Web sites contain a wealth of information on a wide variety of topics. Depending on the level of government, you can use these sites to research trends, statistics, regulations, laws and bylaws, patents, and trademarks. Most government sites also offer articles, papers, essays, and learning kits.

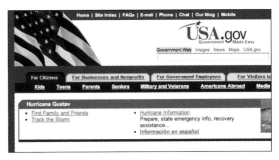

Find People

If you are trying to find a person, the Web has hundreds of sites that enable you to search for phone numbers (such as the Yellow Pages at www.yellowpages.com), postal addresses (such as Addresses.com), e-mail addresses (such as Bigfoot at www.bigfoot.com), and old classmates (such as Classmates.com).

Genealogy

If you are trying to find your ancestors, the Web boasts hundreds of genealogy sites. Either you can search directly using online resources such as birth and death records, or you can use dedicated genealogy sites such as Ancestry.com and Genealogy.com.

Ask an Expert

Hundreds of millions of people access the Web, and many of them are experts on one or more topics. You can find many of these experts at "Ask an Expert" sites that enable you to pose questions that experts in the field will answer. Although some sites require a fee, many sites are free, including AllExperts (www.allexperts.com) and Yahoo! Answers (answers.yahoo.com).

Socialize on the Web

You might not think of the Web as a social medium because people usually cannot see or hear each other. However, the technologies that animate the Web also create new ways to make contact with other people online. As a result, the Web offers many opportunities to socialize.

The social side of the Web is both large and varied, and it has something for everyone, whether you are looking for a friend or a date, or you just want some good conversation.

However, you should supervise all online socializing done by children, and do not give out personal information to strangers.

Meet Friends

If you are looking to meet new friends, either for the social contact or to expand your network, the Web has many sites to check out. These sites include Make Friends Online (www.makefriendsonline.com), Friend Finder (www.friendfinder.com), and Sooper Friends (www.sooperfriends.com). See also the social networking sites that I discuss in Chapter 8.

Find a Date

Most friend-related sites also double as date finders, but there are also hundreds of online dating services that cater to all kinds of people looking for all kinds of relationships. Two of the most popular online dating sites are Lavalife (www.lavalife.com) and Match.com. There are also many sites devoted to specific types of people and relationships, such as JDate (www.jdate.com) which caters to Jewish singles.

Locate a Pen Pal

In the real world, a pen pal is a person with whom you exchange letters. In the online world, a pen pal is someone with whom you exchange e-mail messages. Because e-mails are typed, online pen pals are sometimes called *keypals*. You can use the Web to find online pen pals, particularly for children. For example, see KeyPals Club International (kci.the-protagonist.net) and ePALS (www.epals.com).

Join a Club

The Web is home to many online equivalents of offline clubs such as book clubs and gardening clubs. Whatever your topic of interest, run a Web search on the name of your topic followed by the word "clubs" and you should find some sites of interest. You can also check out some sites that house various clubs and groups, such as Yahoo! Groups (groups.yahoo.com), MSN Groups (groups.msn.com), and Google Groups (groups.google.com).

Register with a Site

If you come across a Web site that interests you, check to see if the site enables you to register. In most cases, this registration enables you to participate in the site's social features, which might include one or more discussion boards, chat rooms, member-to-member communications, blog comments, and more.

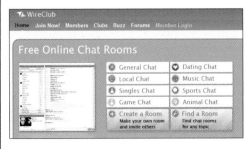

Discussion Boards

Many Web sites offer *discussion boards*, which are also called *message boards* or *forums.* These sections within the site enable visitors to post messages that appear on the site for others to see and reply to. Some discussion boards deal with the site or company, such as the discussion boards on the eBay site (www.ebay.com), whereas others cover a particular subject, such as the numerous gardening forums hosted on GardenWeb (www.gardenweb.com).

Chat Rooms

A *chat room* is a section on a Web site in which visitors can exchange typed messages in real time. Depending on the popularity of the site, a chat room can contain anywhere from a few people chatting to a few dozen. Many chat services also enable you to switch to a "private" chat room for one-on-one discussions.

Play Games Online

If you play video games, then you may be used to playing them by installing programs on your computer or on a dedicated game console. However, the Web is home to many games that you can play online.

There are many Web sites dedicated to online gaming, and you can find games in a wide variety of genres: action, sports, puzzle, arcade, board, word, and more.

You can play games by yourself, against an online opponent, or against many other people. Many online games are free, but in some cases you may need to pay for a game, or pay a fee to access an online gaming site.

Requirements

You can play many online games using just your Web browser. However, to get the most out of your online gaming, you usually need to install some kind of software either on your computer or as a Web browser add-in. The two most common add-ins that online games require are Shockwave (get.adobe.com/shockwave) and Flash (www.adobe.com/products/flashplayer).

Game Sites

The easiest way to play online games is to access one of the many game sites on the Web. Many of these sites are free, but some require a monthly fee to access the games. Some recommended game sites are Miniclip (www.miniclip.com), uclick Games (www.uclickgames.com), OnlineGames.Net (www.onlinegames.net), MSN Games (zone.msn.com), and Yahoo! Games (games.yahoo.com).

Game Consoles

All the major game consoles maintain Web sites that enable you to take your console gaming online. For Microsoft's Xbox gaming console, see the Xbox Live site (www.xbox.com/live). For Sony's PlayStation, see PlayStation.com (www.us.playstation.com). For Nintendo's Wii, see the Global Wii Experience Website (us.wii.com).

MMOG

An MMOG is a massively multiplayer online game, and it refers to a Web site that creates a virtual world where a large number of players — usually hundreds or even thousands of users — compete against and with each other. There are many different types of MMOG, including strategy (for example, Shattered Galaxy; www.sgalaxy.com), racing (such as Drift City; drift.ijji.com), combat (such as World War II Online; www.battlegroundeurope.com), and virtual worlds (such as Second Life; www.secondlife.com).

MMORPG

An MMORPG is a massively multiplayer online role playing game, which is a type of MMOG in which each player assumes a character for the duration of the game. Some popular MMORPGs are World of Warcraft (www.worldofwarcraft.com), Everquest (everquest.station.sony.com), The Lord of the Rings Online (www.lotro.com), Lineage II (www.lineage2.com), and EVE Online (www.eve-online.com).

MUD

A MUD is a multi-user domain (or dungeon), a text-based game that takes place in a simulated fantasy world. That world supports many players at once, and each player is given text that explains the current surroundings and players, and the player types commands to react to and move around in the world. As with MMORPGs, MUD players usually assume a role during the game. Popular MUDs include 3Kingdoms (3k.org), Aardwolf (www.aardwolf.com), and Dark and Shattered Lands (www.dsl-mud.org).

Welcome to the World of 3Kingdoms!

Interactive Fiction

iFiction

Infocom

You step out of the Elevator into the reception area for Infocom, Inc. There is a with doors recedes into the distance. Each door has a sign describing a game tha the doors are locked tight. You are greeted warmly by a man named Laird, acco mentions that they are having an open house, and invites you to look around in th

An interactive fiction game is one that takes place in a text-based fantasy world. Unlike a MUD, an interactive fiction world includes only one player. The player reads about his or her current surroundings and then is given choices about what to do; the choice the player makes determines what happens next. With these choices, the player weaves a story where the object is to solve a puzzle or meet some other goal. To get started, see iFiction (www.ifiction.org).

Bank and Invest on the Web

The Web is home to many financial sites that enable you to do your banking and investing. Banking online is much more convenient and much less time-consuming than doing it in person. Online banking is extremely secure because all modern browsers support robust security protocols that ensure your financial data remains safe.

Investing online makes sense because you can use the Web's resources to research your investments. Many sites also enable you to set up online portfolios to track your investments. You can also use online brokerages to buy and sell securities from the convenience of your home.

Online Banking

Most banks now offer online versions that you can access through your Web browser to check account balances, transfer funds, view previous transactions, order checks, arrange loans, and more. There are also *virtual banks* that exist only online, including eBank (www.ebank.com), ING Direct (www.ingdirect.com), and Bank of Internet (www.bankofinternet.com). Before choosing an online bank, check that it is FDIC insured, and research the transaction fees.

Online Bill Paying

Almost all online banks offer the option to pay your bills electronically. However, if you elect not to do your banking on the Web, you can still pay your bills online using a site that offers bill payment services. Examples include Paytrust (www.paytrust.com), MyCheckFree (www.mycheckfree.com), and MSN Bill Pay (billpay.msn.com).

Bank-Related Phishing

Beware of e-mail messages that appear to come from a bank or credit union. The message will tell you that you have a problem with your account and will provide a link to a site that enables you to the fix the "problem." However, this is a phishing scam attempting to trick you into providing your bank login data. No reputable financial institution ever solicits login details or other sensitive data via e-mail.

Financial News

Good investing means staying on top of the latest financial and company news, and the Web is home to many sites that offer such news. These sites include The Motley Fool (www.fool.com), Yahoo! Finance (finance.yahoo.com), CNN Money (money.cnn.com), MarketWatch (www.marketwatch.com), and MSN Money (moneycentral. msn.com). A good source of links to all things financial is InvestorLinks (www.investorlinks.com).

Stock Quotes

Most of the financial news sites also offer stock quotes, most of which are delayed (usually by 15 or 20 minutes), but some are shown in real-time (such as Yahoo! Finance quotes). Other online sites for stock quotes are Google Finance (finance.google.com), Quote.com (www.quote.com), and PCQuote (www.pcquote.com).

Company Research

Before making investment decisions, it is a good idea to research the companies you are interested in. The Web is the ideal place for such research. You can either run a Web search on the company name, or you can use Web sites that are devoted to providing company data. These include the Securities and Exchange Commission's EDGAR Database (www.sec.gov/edgar/searchedgar/webusers.htm), FreeEdgar (www.freeedgar.com), Corporate Information (www. corporateinformation.com), and Hoovers (www.hoovers.com).

Online Brokerages

You can buy and sell stock, bonds, mutual funds, options, and other securities using an online brokerage. When researching brokerages, check the minimum amount required to open an account, and compare the trade commissions. Some of the more popular online brokerages are Fidelity (www.fidelity.com), Charles Schwab (www. schwab.com), TD Ameritrade (www.tdameritrade.com), Merrill Lynch Direct (www.mldirect.com), and ShareBuilder (www.sharebuilder.com).

Book a Trip Using the Web

Until recently it was common practice to use a travel agent to arrange a vacation or other trip. Now travel agents are a vanishing breed because many travelers find it easier and cheaper to research and book a trip using the Web's many travel-related resources.

You can use the Web to visit the sites maintained by airlines, hotels, and rental agencies. You can see reviews of places to stay, compare prices, and research possible destinations. Once you know where you want to go, you can use the Web to book the complete trip, including the flight, accommodations, and car rental.

General Travel Sites

There are many general-purpose travel sites on the Web. These sites enable you to research and book complete trips, from the flight to the hotel to the car rental, and they usually also include vacation packages. The top travel sites are Expedia (www.expedia.com), Travelocity (www.travelocity.com), Yahoo! Travel (travel.yahoo.com), and Orbitz (www.orbitz.com).

Travel Search Engines

One of the best ways to get familiar with current airfare and hotel availability and pricing is to use a travel search engine. These search engines look for the best deals by scouring general travel sites, as well as airline and hotel sites. Useful travel search engines are Yahoo! FareChase (farechase.yahoo.com), Live Search Farecast (farecast.live.com), Kayak (www.kayak.com), and FareCompare (www.farecompare.com).

Bidding Sites

If you are looking for the cheapest airfare or hotel rate, or if you have a specific budget in mind, consider using a travel bidding site. With these sites you say what you are willing to pay, and the site tries to find a matching flight or hotel. Some travel bidding sites are Hotwire (www.hotwire.com) and Priceline (www.priceline.com).

Direct Reservations

Because most travel sites charge a fee to book your travel, you can often get the best price by dealing directly with an airline, hotel, or car rental agency. All major travel operations maintain Web sites that enable you to examine their offerings and make bookings. Be sure to look for sales and other special deals to get the best price.

Trip Research

The general travel sites such as Expedia and Travelocity offer information about destinations, so you can use them as part of your research. It is also a good idea to visit the online tourist/visitor information sites maintained by most countries and cities. Travel guide sites such as Frommer's (www.frommers.com), Lonely Planet (www.lonelyplanet.com), and Fodors (www.fodors.com) also offer lots of great information.

Mapping Services

With your trip booked, you can use mapping sites to learn more about your destination and get directions to popular places. The Web's main mapping services are Google Maps (maps.google.com), MapQuest (www.mapquest.com), and Yahoo! Maps (maps.yahoo.com). For more details on using the Web's mapping services, see Chapter 7.

Find a Job on the Web

Whether you are looking for your first job or just for a better job, the Web offers tons of resources that can help.

If you are just starting out, or if your job search skills are rusty, the Web has many sites that offer job search tips, resume ideas, cover letter advice, and more. You can also use the Web to research careers and employers.

When you are ready to look for a job, the Web has many sites to check out. These include job sites run by employers; job boards that aggregate jobs from many companies; and specialty sites for things like job sharing, seasonal work, and part-time work.

Job Search Advice

The Web is home to many sites that offer advice on various aspects of the job search, including finding the right career, writing a resume and cover letter, and surveys of salaries and job prospects in different sectors. Some sites to check out are The Wall Street Journal's CareerJournal (online.wsj.com/careers), JobStar (www.jobstar.org), The Career Key (www.careerkey.org), and Job Hunter's Bible (www.jobhuntersbible.com).

Researching Occupations

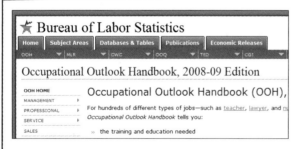

If you are looking for a particular type of job, it helps to know as much as possible about that occupation, including the background required, what the job entails, and what the outlook is for salaries and job prospects. In the U.S., check out the Bureau of Labor Statistics' Occupational Outlook Handbook (www.bls.gov/oco). In Canada, see the federal government's Labour Market Information site (www.labourmarketinformation.ca).

Aptitude Testing

Before deciding on a particular career path, it helps to know if you are suited to that occupation. Several online sites offer career testing. These sites include Career Games (www.careergames.com), The Career Key (www.careerkey.org), Career Planner (www.careerplanner.com), and Career Zone (www.nycareerzone.org).

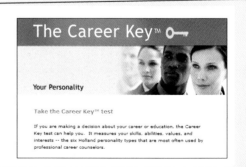

Employer Sites

If there is a particular company you would like to work for, you should visit that company's Web site and see what jobs it is currently advertising. Some employers post job vacancies *only* on their Web site, so you should always visit several employer sites during your search. Look for links with names such as Employment, Careers, or Jobs.

Job Boards

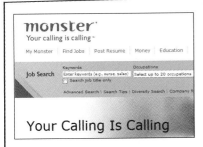

A *job board* is an employment site that lists a large number of jobs from many different employers and industries. The most popular job boards are Monster (www.monster.com), craigslist (www.craigslist.org), Career Builder (www.careerbuilder.com), Yahoo! HotJobs (hotjobs.yahoo.com), and FlipDog (www.flipdog.com). Canadians should also try Workopolis (www.workopolis.com).

Government Jobs

Governments are one of the biggest employers, so you should not overlook them in your job search. Governments at all levels post jobs on the Web, so try searching the government's main site for job listings. See also USAJOBS (www.usajobs.gov), GovernmentJobs (www.governmentjobs.com), and the Canadian federal government jobs site (jobs.gc.ca).

Specialty Job Sites

If full-time work is not for you, there are many opportunities for alternative employment arrangements such as job sharing, freelancing, working from home, side jobs, and part-time work. Some sites that specialize in these types of jobs are Work Options (www.workoptions.com), Woman's Work (www.womans-work.com), Guru.com, and iFreelance (www.ifreelance.com). See also the discussion of the LinkedIn social networking site in Chapter 8.

Explore Sites for Kids

The Web is home to a huge number of sites for kids of all ages. Whether you are introducing your youngest to the Internet, looking to keep a child occupied for a while, or are looking for entertainment for a bored teen, the Web has sites that can help.

Many kid-related sites are all about having fun with activities, puzzles, quizzes, games, and more. However, the Web has all kinds of sites that enable your child to learn about a variety of topics, including animals, dinosaurs, science, art, history, and much more.

Fun

Comic Zone (www.unitedmedia.com/comics)

Crayola (www.crayola.com)

FamilyFun (familyfun.go.com)

Funology (www.funology.com)

Seussville (www.seussville.com)

Games

Candystand (www.candystand.com)

Crazy Bone (www.crazybone.com)

MazeWorks (www.mazeworks.com)

Pojo (www.pojo.com)

Prongo (www.prongo.com)

Puzzle Choice (www.puzzlechoice.com)

Quiz Hub (www.quizhub.com)

For Girls

A Girl's World (www.agirlsworld.com)

Girl Zone (www.girlzone.com)

GirlSense (www.girlsense.com)

Go Girls Only (www.gogirlsonly.org)

gURL (www.gurl.com)

SmartGirl (www.smartgirl.org)

Animals

Animaland (www.animaland.org)

Animal Corner! (www.animalcorner.co.uk)

National Wildlife Federation (www.nwf.org/kids)

Insectlopedia (www.insectclopedia.com)

Kids' Planet (www.kidsplanet.org)

Kids Go Wild (www.kidsgowild.com)

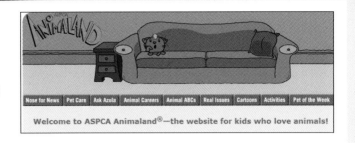

Welcome to ASPCA Animaland®—the website for kids who love animals!

Dinosaurs

The Dino Dictionary (www.dinodictionary.com)

The Dinosauria (www.ucmp.berkeley.edu/diapsids/dinosaur.html)

Download-a-Dinosaur (www.rain.org/ ~ philfear/download-a-dinosaur.html)

Science and Nature

Bill Nye the Science Guy (www.billnye.com)

EcoKids (www.ecokids.ca)

Grossology (www.grossology.org)

KidsHealth (www.kidshealth.org)

Kids' Planet (www.kidsplanet.org)

WhyFiles (www.whyfiles.org)

Yuckiest Site on the Internet (www.yucky.com)

General

Kids' Space (kids-space.org)

KidsCom (www.kidscom.com)

Kidsites (www.kidsites.org)

MaMaMedia (www.mamamedia.com)

PBS for Kids (www.pbskids.org)

Sports Illustrated for Kids (www.sikids.com)

Yahoo! Kids (kids.yahoo.com)

Create Your Own Web Site

Instead of just reading the Web sites created by companies, organizations, and individuals, you can join in by creating your own site.

Once you have decided on a topic, you create your own Web site by building Web pages on your computer. You build these pages either by hand or by using a Web page editor. You then publish your pages on the Web.

To publish your Web pages, you need to set up an account with a *Web hosting provider*, which is a company that offers space to store Web pages, as well as a Web server to display your pages to visitors who request them.

Choose a Topic

The most successful personal Web sites are those that focus on one or two topics. If you have recently taken a trip, or if you have a hobby, a passion, a favorite sport, artistic talent, or something else that you want to share with the world, build your site around that topic. Many people also build Web sites to share family news and photos with friends and other family members.

Learn HTML and CSS

You can build pages yourself using a text editor — such as the Notepad program that comes with Windows, or the TextEdit program that comes with Mac OS X. All Web pages are composed of text interspersed with Hypertext Markup Language (HTML) codes that define how you want the page laid out, and Cascading Style Sheets (CSS) codes that define how you want the text and page to look.

Web Page Editor

If you do not want to learn HTML and CSS, you can build your Web pages using a program called a Web page editor, which is also called an HTML editor. Popular Web page editors include CoffeeCup, available from www.coffeecup.com, and Macromedia HomeSite, available from www.adobe.com/products/homesite. You can also use Microsoft Word to build a Web page.

Choose a Web-Hosting Provider

Storage Space

Storage space refers to the amount of room allotted to you on the host's Web server to store your files. If you have a 1MB limit, then you cannot store more than 1MB worth of files on the server. HTML files are not big, but graphic files can be, and so you need to watch your limit. Generally, the more you pay for a host, the more storage space you acquire.

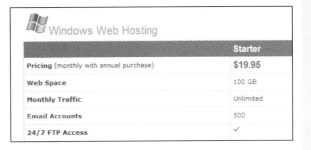

Bandwidth

Bandwidth is a measure of how much of your data the server sends out. For example, if you have a page that is 10KB, including images, and ten people access the page (either at the same time or over a period of time), the total bandwidth is 100KB. Most hosts give you a bandwidth limit (or *cap*), which is usually a specified number of megabytes or gigabytes per month.

Domain Name

A *domain name* is a general Internet address, such as wiley.com or whitehouse.gov. Most Web hosts supply a domain name, but you can also purchase your own domain name using a site such as GoDaddy.com. Two types of domain names are available. One type is a regular domain name, such as mydomain.com. The other type is a subdomain name, such as mydomain.webhostdomain.com, where "webhostdomain.com" is the domain name of the Web hosting company.

Other Features

Other features to look for when researching your Web hosting provider are the number of e-mail accounts provided; scripts that enable you to add advanced features such as forms; a high *uptime* value, which refers to the percentage of time the host's server is up and serving (the best hosts have uptime numbers over 99 percent); and free tech support, ideally available 24 hours a day, seven days a week.

Chapter 7

Working with Internet Media

Web sites, blogs, e-mail, and instant messaging showcase the text side of the Internet, and most Web surfing excursions require quite a bit of reading. However, the Internet has plenty of non-text treats to stimulate your senses.

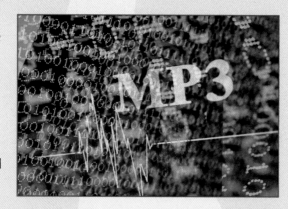

For your ears, you can download music, subscribe to podcasts, tune in to Internet-based radio stations, and listen to streaming audio.

For your eyes, you can flip through the photos that people are sharing, view streaming video, check out what everyone's watching on the YouTube site, and learn more about a place by using online maps and satellite images.

Get Music over the Internet

If you enjoy listening to music while using your computer, or if you want to expand your music collection, the Internet is home to many sites that offer music, and those sites enable you to save music to your computer.

From there, you can listen to the music on your computer, add it to a digital music player, such as an iPod, or copy the music to a disc for playback in a CD player.

In this section, you learn about getting music in the form of digital music files. Later in this chapter you learn how to get music via Internet radio stations and streaming audio.

Digital Music Files

A *digital music file* is a data file that, in most cases, contains a single song or album track. When you purchase a song from an online music store or click a link to a free song, the associated digital music file is downloaded to your computer. This enables you to play the song on your computer, add the song to an iPod or other music device, or burn the song to a recordable CD.

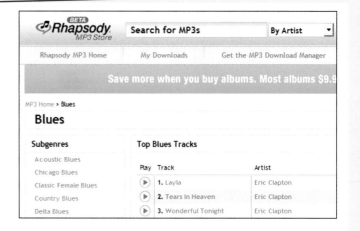

MP3

The Motion Picture Experts Group Audio Level 3, or MP3, is one of the most popular music file formats. It compresses digital music by removing extraneous sounds that are not normally detected by the human ear. This results in high-quality music files that are one-tenth the size of uncompressed music, thus making MP3s ideal for downloading and storing on digital audio players (which are frequently called *MP3 players*, even when they support other audio formats).

Other Music Formats

Besides MP3, digital music comes in a number of other file formats. The most popular of these is Windows Media Audio (WMA), which produces audio files with the same quality as MP3, but that are compressed to about half the size. WMA is often used for digital audio player storage because it can fit twice the number of songs as MP3. On the Mac and in Apple's iTunes digital music player, the most popular format is Advanced Audio Coding (AAC).

Online Music Store

The easiest way to download digital music files is to use an online music store. Most stores sell both individual songs — usually for less than a dollar — and entire albums. The most popular online music stores are iTunes (see www.apple.com/itunes to download the iTunes software), eMusic (www.emusic.com), and Spiralfrog (www.spiralfrog.com). See also regular retailers such as Amazon.com.

Online Music Service

With an online music service, you pay a monthly fee that entitles you to download and play songs, often an unlimited number of songs. Note, however, that in most cases you only have access to your songs as long as you maintain your subscription. Popular online music services are Rhapsody (www.rhapsody.com), Napster (www.napster.com), and Zune Marketplace (www.zune.net).

Digital Rights Management

Some digital audio content is in the public domain, which means that you can use it without paying for it. However, most digital audio content — particularly commercial music — is protected by copyright. This means that legally you should not play the audio unless you get permission or pay a fee. In either case, you are given a digital license that allows you to play the audio file, and that may also place restrictions on whether you can copy the file to devices other than your computer.

Listening to Music

To listen to your digital music files, you need a software program called a digital music player. Windows PCs come with Windows Media Player; Macs come with iTunes. You can also install third-party programs such as RealPlayer (www.real.com), Winamp (www.winamp.com), and iTunes for Windows (www.apple.com/itunes).

Subscribe to a Podcast

A *podcast* is an audio feed — or sometimes a feed that combines both audio and video — that a publisher updates regularly with new episodes. The easiest way to get each episode is to subscribe to the podcast using iTunes. This ensures that iTunes automatically downloads each new episode to your iTunes Library. You can subscribe to podcasts either directly via the publisher's Web site, or via the iTunes Store.

Many publishers make their podcasts available in the MP3 audio format. This enables you to download the podcast to your computer and then listen to it using a digital music player.

Subscribe to a Podcast

SUBSCRIBE TO A PODCAST ON THE WEB

1 Use your Web browser to navigate to the podcast's home page.

2 Click the **Subscribe in iTunes** link.

Note: In some cases, the link is called Add to iTunes or simply iTunes.

● If an MP3 version exists, click the link to download the file to your computer.

● iTunes begins downloading the available episodes.

● The podcast subscription appears in the Library's Podcasts category.

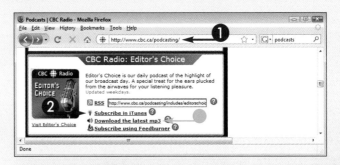

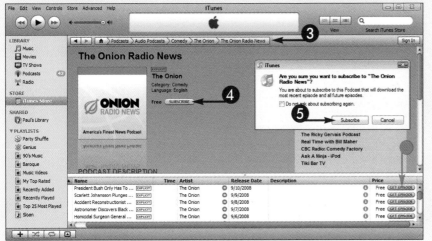

SUBSCRIBE TO A PODCAST USING THE ITUNES STORE

1 Click **iTunes Store**.

2 Click **Podcasts**.

3 Locate the podcast you want to subscribe to.

Note: Use categories such as Comedy and subcategories such as The Onion to locate podcasts.

4 Click **Subscribe**.

● If you just want to listen to one episode before subscribing, click **Get Episode**, instead.

iTunes asks you to confirm.

5 Click **Subscribe**.

iTunes adds the subscription to the Podcasts category of the Library.

Simplify It

What do I do if the podcast Web site does not have an iTunes link?
Look for a link to an MP3 file, instead. If there is no MP3 link, you can subscribe to the podcast by telling iTunes the address of the podcast's feed. Follow these steps:

1 On the podcast Web site, copy the address of the podcast feed.

2 In iTunes, click **Advanced**.

3 Click **Subscribe to Podcast**.

The Subscribe to Podcast dialog box appears.

4 Use the **URL** text box to paste (or type) the address of the podcast feed.

5 Click **OK**.

iTunes downloads the available episodes and adds the subscription to the Podcasts category of the Library.

Listen to Internet Radio

The Internet offers many radio stations that you can listen to. Like a regular radio station, an Internet radio station broadcasts a constant audio stream, except you access the audio online instead of over the air.

You can access Internet radio sites directly and listen to the audio stream using a player the site provides. Many over-the-air radio stations

also stream their live broadcasts from their home pages.

You can also get Internet radio using Windows Media Player or iTunes. Both programs have lists of online radio stations, so it is often easier to use Media Player or iTunes to listen to Internet radio.

LISTEN TO INTERNET RADIO WITH MEDIA PLAYER

1 Click **Media Guide**.

Media Player connects to WindowsMedia.com.

2 Click **Radio**.

Media Player displays a list of radio genres.

3 Click the genre you want to listen to.

Media Player displays a list of radio station streams in the genre.

● If you want to choose a different genre, click ⊡.

4 Click ⊻ to see details about a station (⊻ changes to ⊼).

5 Click **Play**.

For some stations, Media Player asks if you want to play enhanced content.

6 Click **Yes**.

Media Player plays the radio station stream.

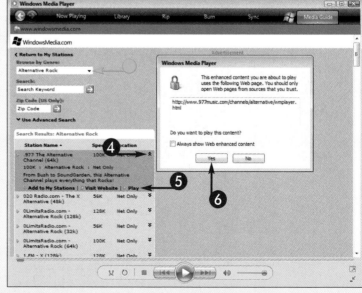

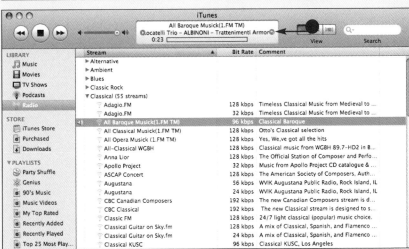

LISTEN TO INTERNET RADIO WITH ITUNES

1 Click **Radio**.

iTunes displays a list of radio genres.

2 Click ▶ to open the genre you want to work with (▶ changes to ▼).

iTunes displays a list of radio station streams in the genre.

3 Double-click the radio station stream you want to listen to.

iTunes plays the radio station stream.

● The name of the station and the name of the currently playing track usually appear here.

Simplify It

Is it possible to save or record a song from a radio station stream?	**What do the numbers in Media Player's Speed column and iTunes' Bit Rate column refer to?**
Generally, no, because an Internet radio stream is "listen-only." Neither Media Player nor iTunes give you any way to save the stream to your hard disk or to record the stream as it plays. There are third-party programs available on the Internet that enable you to record radio. However, this is usually a copyright violation, so check the radio station usage guidelines before attempting to record the station.	The speed or bit rate is measured in kilobits per second (Kbps) and is the rate at which the Internet radio station broadcasts the stream. The higher the rate, the better the music quality, but higher rates also require a fast Internet connection. Some stations offer multiple bit rates, so if a stream is choppy or distorted, try listening to a lower bit rate stream.

Share Photos on the Web

Do you take digital photographs? If so, then you might want to share some or all of them with friends, family, and even complete strangers.

You can do this by signing up with a photo sharing site, which is a Web site that enables you to upload digital photos that can then be viewed, rated, tagged, and commented upon by other people.

Most photo sharing sites offer free accounts, but in many cases you can also upgrade to a paid account to get more storage space and more features.

Storage

The most important consideration when deciding which photo sharing site to use is how much storage space you get on the site. Because digital photos are often quite large, the more storage space you have, the more photos you can upload to the site. For free accounts, most photo sharing sites offer between 100MB and 1GB of storage. Almost all sites also enable you to purchase more storage space.

Features

Besides storage space, all photo sharing sites offer several features and you should compare these features before creating an account. The most common features are the ability to edit your photos, order prints, and create calendars and greeting cards using your photos. It is also useful to have multiple methods that you can use to upload photos, such as via the Web, via e-mail, and via programs such as iPhoto.

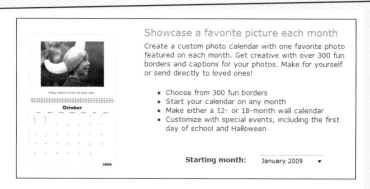

Showcase a favorite picture each month

Create a custom photo calendar with one favorite photo featured on each month. Get creative with over 300 fun borders and captions for your photos. Make for yourself or send directly to loved ones!

- Choose from 300 fun borders
- Start your calendar on any month
- Make either a 12- or 18-month wall calendar
- Customize with special events, including the first day of school and Halloween

Starting month: January 2009   ▼

Flickr

Flickr (www.flickr.com) is currently the most popular of the photo sharing sites. You can edit your photos, organize them into albums (called *sets*), create cards and books, and control who can view your photos. A free Flickr account enables you to upload 100MB of photos each month, and photo displays are limited to the most recent 200 images. For $24.95 per year, you can upgrade to a Pro account that offers unlimited uploads and storage.

Picasa Web Albums

Picasa Web Albums (picasaweb.google.com) is Google's photo sharing site. People can subscribe to your photo albums, and you can control whether people can download and create prints from your photos. A free Picasa account gives you 1GB of storage space. You can upgrade your storage for a fee ranging from $20 per year for 10GB to $500 per year for 400GB.

Shutterfly

Shutterfly (www.shutterfly.com) is a popular photo sharing site that specializes in creating gift items from your photos. Gifts include greeting cards, calendars, books, posters, jewelry, coffee cups, and more. Your free account offers unlimited storage, and you can share some or all of your photos with other users.

Fotolog

Fotolog (www.fotolog.com) enables you to create a Web page centered around the photos that you upload. Fotolog is a kind of blog (see Chapter 13) in that you do not upload all of your digital photos. Instead, with Fotolog you just upload your best photos so your Fotolog page becomes a daily log of the photos you most want to share with the world. A free Fotolog account allows one upload per day. You can upgrade to a Gold Camera account for about $5 per month, and that entitles you to upload as many as six photos per day.

Photobucket

Photobucket (www.photobucket.com) is a popular photo sharing site that enables you to edit your photos, organize them into albums, create slide shows, and control who can view your photos. You can also turn your photos into greeting cards, posters, prints, books, and other merchandise. With a free Photobucket account, you get 1GB of storage space, but you can upgrade to a Pro account for $39.95 per year to get 10GB of space.

Access Streaming Media

Streaming media refers to audio or video data broadcast continuously from a Web site. You use a software program on your computer to initiate or connect to the stream and listen to or view the media.

Unlike a digital audio or video file, you cannot save a media stream to your computer's hard disk for later playback. Instead, a media stream is more like a radio or television signal. In the same way that you use a radio receiver or a TV set to tune in to a signal, you use a media player program on your computer to tune in to a media stream.

On Demand Streaming

There are two types of media streaming: on demand and live. On demand media streaming means that the stream resides on a Web server and is available any time. You use your Web browser or a media player program to locate the media stream you want, and then initiate the stream. In many cases you can manipulate the stream by pausing it, rewinding it, and so on. On demand steaming is similar to pay-per-view TV programming, although many streams are free.

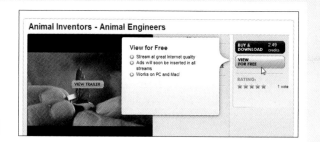

Live Streaming

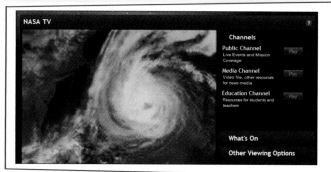

Live media streaming means that the stream is broadcast from a Web server at a particular time, and you use your Web browser or a media player program to access the stream as it plays. You cannot rewind or fast-forward a live media stream. Live streaming is similar to standard television and radio where shows are broadcast at a set time, and you tune it to the show you want to watch.

Streaming Media Player

Although some streaming media does not require any special software beyond your Web browser, many streams require a media player. Some streams work only with a specific media player. For example, streams based on the QuickTime format require Apple's QuickTime player. Other streaming media players include Windows Media Player, iTunes, RealPlayer (www.real.com), Flash Player (www.adobe.com), and Winamp (www.winamp.com). Some sites use a proprietary media player like the one shown here from the Classical.com site.

Streaming Audio

The most common form of streaming audio is an Internet radio station, as discussed in the "Listen to Internet Radio" section. Also, subscription music sites use streaming audio to deliver their songs (see "Get Music over the Internet"). The most common streaming audio formats are Windows Media (use Windows Media Player or RealPlayer), QuickTime (QuickTime player), Real (RealPlayer), Ogg Vorbis (Winamp), and MP3 (any player).

Streaming Video

Streaming video is on demand or live audiovisual content, including live video feeds (for example, see UStream at www.ustream.tv), video clips (such as YouTube; see "Watch and Upload YouTube Videos"), TV shows, and movies. The most common streaming video formats are Flash Video (any player), Windows Media (use Windows Media Player or RealPlayer), QuickTime (QuickTime player), Real (RealPlayer), and MP4 (any player). You need a fast Internet connection to watch streaming video.

Streaming TV Sites

Many news networks stream live video feeds, including CNN (www.cnn.com), MSNBC (www.msnbc.msn.com), and Fox News (www.foxnews.com). Many other networks also make previously aired episodes available, including PBS (www.pbs.org) and MTV (www.mtv.com). Many NBC and Fox shows are available at Hulu (www.hulu.com).

Streaming Movie Sites

There are many Internet sites that offer streaming movies, but many of them are illegal, so be careful. Legitimate streaming movie sites include Netflix (www.netflix.com), CinemaNow (www.cinemanow.com), factualTV (www.factualtv.com), Hulu (www.hulu.com), MovieFlix (www.movieflix.com), and Movielink (www.movielink.com).

Watch and Upload YouTube Videos

YouTube is a video sharing service that is one of the most popular sites on the Web. YouTube offers tens of millions of videos from amateur videographers and moviemakers, as well as movie trailers, commercials, clips from TV shows, and more. You use the YouTube site to start a video clip, and YouTube streams the video to your computer.

If you have a digital movie or animation that you would like to share with the world, you can upload the file to YouTube. To upload videos, you need to create a free YouTube account, or sign in with your Google account if you have one.

Watch and Upload YouTube Videos

WATCH A YOUTUBE VIDEO

1 Use your Web browser to navigate to the YouTube site at www.youtube.com.

2 Click **Videos**.

3 Click a category.

4 Click the video you want to watch.

● YouTube begins playing the video.

● Click **Pause** (⏸) to pause the video stream (⏸ changes to ▶).

Note: Click ▶ to resume playing the video.

● Click and drag the slider to the left to rewind, or to the right to fast-forward.

● To adjust the volume, position your mouse over the **Volume** icon (🔊) and then click and drag the slider that appears.

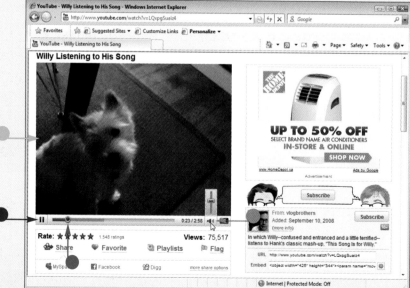

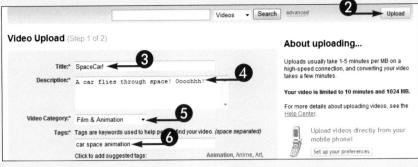

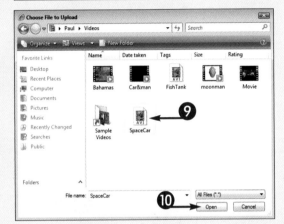

UPLOAD A YOUTUBE VIDEO

① Sign in to your YouTube account.

② Click **Upload**.

③ Type a title for your video.

④ Type a description.

⑤ Click 🔽 and then click a video category.

⑥ Type one or more keywords.

⑦ Click **Upload a video** at the bottom of the window (not shown).

⑧ Click **Browse**.

⑨ Click the video file.

⑩ Click **Open**.

⑪ Click **Upload Video**.

How can I embed a YouTube video on one of my Web pages?

① In YouTube, click the video you want to embed on your page.

② Click inside the **Embed** text box to the right of the video.

The Web browser automatically selects all the text, which is the code you use to embed the video.

③ Press `Ctrl` + `C` (or `⌘` + `C` on a Mac) to copy the code.

④ Open your Web page for editing.

⑤ Position the cursor where you want the video to appear.

⑥ Press `Ctrl` + `V` (or `⌘` + `V` on a Mac).

Your computer pastes the code into the page.

Get Directions with Google Maps

When you are out in the real world, it can be difficult to navigate your way to an unfamiliar destination. The old-fashioned solution is to pull out a paper map, but if you have Internet access, a much better solution is to use the Google Maps service.

Google Maps is a giant geographical database that covers most cities and towns, particularly in North America. Google Maps can not only show you a map of a particular place, it also allows you to zoom in to get a more detailed look. More importantly, Google Maps can also give you street-by-street, turn-by-turn instructions on how to get to a particular location.

Get Directions with Google Maps

① Use your Web browser to navigate to the Google Maps site at maps.google.com.

② Type the name or address of the location you want to visit.

③ Click **Search Maps**.

Google Maps displays a map of the city or town.

● Google Maps shows you the location you specified.

● Use these controls to zoom in and out of the map.

● Use these controls to pan the map east, west, north, and south.

④ Click **Get directions**.

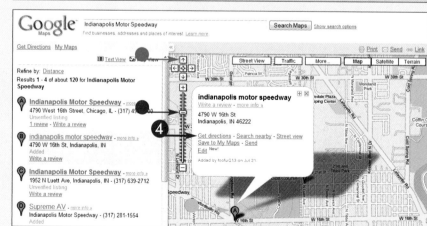

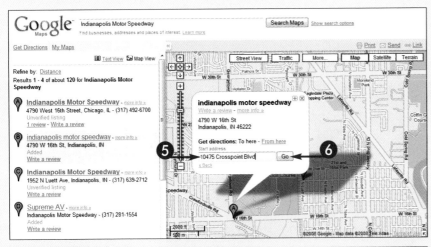

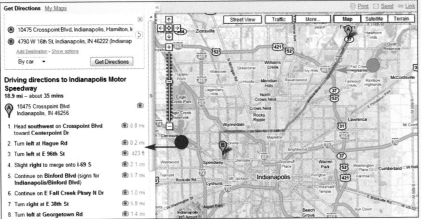

Google Maps asks you for the address of your starting point.

⑤ Type your starting address.

⑥ Click **Go**.

● Google Maps displays the route.

● Google Maps provides specific directions.

Simplify It

Is there a way to configure Google Maps to use my home address as the starting point?
Yes. First, use your Web browser to navigate to the Google Maps site at maps.google.com. Click the **Set default location** link. In the **Set default location** text box, type your home address, and then click **Save**. To get directions from your home to some destination, return to maps.google.com and click the **Get Directions** link. Your home address appears automatically in the **A** text box. Type the destination in the **B** text box, and then click **Get Directions**.

Is there a way to avoid traffic, highways, and toll booths in the directions?
Yes, if you live in a major U.S. city. To see the current traffic conditions, click the **Traffic** button at the top of the map. Slow-moving routes are shown in red and fast-moving routes in green. Click the **Show options** link and then click **Avoid highways** (◎ changes to ◉) or **Avoid tolls** (◎ changes to ◉) to adjust the route to bypass these items.

Chapter 8

Social Networking

Social networking refers to a Web service that enables you to connect with people who share similar personal or professional interests. On most social networking sites, the members are connected to each other as friends, friends of friends, and so on.

Social networking is one of the Web's most popular pastimes, with sites such as Facebook and MySpace boasting over 100 million members each. In this chapter you find out what social networking is all about, and you learn about a few of the most popular social networking sites.

Understanding Social Networking

Social networking has been around for only a few years, but it is already the most popular and the most talked about Web pastime. Before you take the social networking plunge, you should understand what social networking is all about.

For example, you should understand the point of social networking, the role of friends in social networks, the types of information and data that people share with those friends, and the privacy and security issues that are related to sharing your data online.

Purpose

There are two main reasons why people use social networking sites. First, social networking sites are an easy and convenient way to keep track of what is going on in the lives of friends, family, and colleagues, particularly people that you do not see regularly. Second, social networking sites are a great way to expand your circle of friends, acquaintances, and business contacts because you can usually see and connect with the friends of your existing friends.

Signing Up

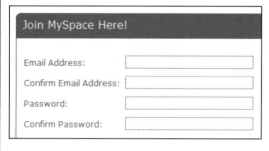

All social networking sites give everyone limited access to the site's features and members. However, if you want to access all the site's features, and in particular if you want to connect with the site's members, then you must sign up for an account. All social networking sites offer free membership, and the sign-up process usually requests a limited amount of personal data, including your name, a display name that others see, your e-mail address, and your location.

Friends

All social networks revolve around the concept of *friends* (sometimes called *connections* or *contacts*). A friend is another member of the same social network that you have established a relationship with. In most cases, you establish this relationship by sending the person a *friend request*. If the other person accepts the request, he or she is added to your list of friends. This enables you to send messages to that person, view that person's profile, and see status updates from that person.

Personal Profile

When you become a member of a social networking site, one of the first things you usually do is fill in your personal profile. The information in this profile varies from site to site, but the data usually includes your interests and hobbies, your current and past jobs, your education, your birthday, your relationship status, and a photo.

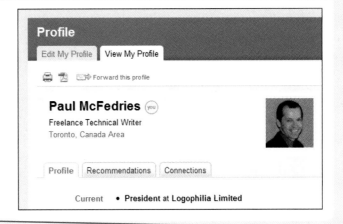

Sharing

Making friends is the "networking" part of social networking, and the "social" part involves sharing information and data with your friends. What and how you share information depends on the site, but in most cases you can share things like updates on your current status or activities, photos, groups on the site that you have joined, blog posts, and links to interesting sites on the Web.

Mobile Updates

If your status changes while you are away from your computer, or if you take an interesting photo when you are traveling, you do not have to wait until you return to your PC to update your social networking account with the new data. Most social networks offer a mobile feature that enables you to send text or photos via your cell phone.

Privacy and Security

If you are concerned about making so much personal information available online, remember that in most cases you can add to your profile only the information that you are comfortable sharing with others. Also, all social networks come with privacy features that enable you to control who gets to see your personal profile.

Discover Facebook

Facebook (www.facebook.com) is one of the most popular social networking sites on the Web, with over 100 million users worldwide. Facebook started in 2004 as a tool for connecting students at Harvard University, but it soon expanded to other universities and then to high school students. In the fall of 2006 Facebook was opened to anyone over the age of 13.

Facebook offers a clean, easy-to-use interface that is the same for every member. Facebook comes with a default set of applications that enable you to post messages and photos, but there are also thousands of third-party applications that you can use to customize your Facebook experience.

Sign Up

Unlike most other Web sites that allow any visitor to see their full content, nonmembers can see only a very limited amount of data on the Facebook site. To see more data and to use the Facebook features, you must sign up for a Facebook account. To sign up, either surf to the Facebook home page at www.facebook.com, or click the **Sign Up** link that appears on most other Facebook pages.

Fill In Your Profile

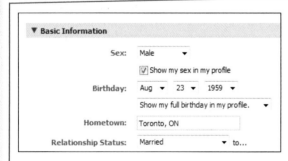

Once your Facebook account is active, log in using your e-mail address and password, click **Profile**, click **Info**, and then click **Edit Information**. Facebook divides your profile into four sections: Basic Information, Personal Information, Contact Information, and Education and Work. For each section, click the section header to open it, enter as much information as you feel comfortable sharing, and then click **Save Changes**. When you are finished, click **Done Editing**.

Make Friends

Like any social networking site, Facebook is all about making friends, so the site gives you a number of ways to add friends to your profile. Click the **Home** tab and then click the **Friend Finder** link. From here, you can access your online address book, upload your computer's contacts, or search for people you know. If you find someone you know, click the **Add as Friend** link and then click **Add Friend**. The other person must then confirm you as a friend.

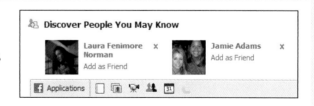

Add Content

You use Facebook by adding content to your profile, and your friends automatically see this content as you add it. Click **Home**, click the **Wall** tab, and then use the links to add the content you want. For example, click **Update Status** to write a short description of what you are doing now; click **Share Link** to give your friends a link to an interesting Web site; click **Add Photos** to upload one or more photos to your profile; click **Add Video** to add a video stream, video file, or YouTube video link; and click **Write Note** to add a short post to your profile.

Connect with a Friend

Your friends keep up with you by having your new content appear in their News Feed tab. You can also connect more directly with a friend. For example, to write on a friend's Wall, click the friend, click the **Wall** tab, click **Write**, and then write your post. You can also "poke" a friend (he or she sees a small icon from you), comment on any new content a friend has added, chat with friends who are online, and send a friend a message.

Work with Applications

The Facebook features that enable you to add photos, videos, notes, and more to your profile are examples of Facebook applications. Facebook comes with lots of built-in applications that you can add, and there are thousands of third-party applications for you to check out. Click **Applications**, click **Edit**, and then click **Browse more applications**.

Change Settings

Facebook enables you to customize your account by offering dozens of settings. For example, position the mouse ⬧ over **Settings** and then click **Account Settings**. You can use the My Account page to change your name, password, security question, Facebook networks, notifications, and Facebook Mobile. To specify how your profile and other data are shared, position the mouse ⬧ over **Settings** and then click **Privacy Settings**.

Take a Tour of MySpace

MySpace (www.myspace.com) is currently the most popular social networking site on the Web, with well over 100 million users worldwide. MySpace was founded in 2003 and was purchased in 2005 by News Corporation.

MySpace allows members to completely customize their own pages, which gives

MySpace a vibrant and often chaotic feel. MySpace specializes in music pages, so it is an excellent place to find new bands. With your own profile, you can share pictures and photo albums, create your own blog, and exchange messages with your friends.

Sign Up

Depending on the settings MySpace users have configured for their account, nonmembers can usually see only a limited amount of data on the MySpace site. To see more data and to use the MySpace features, you must sign up for a MySpace account. To sign up, surf to the MySpace home page at www. myspace.com and click the **Sign Up** link.

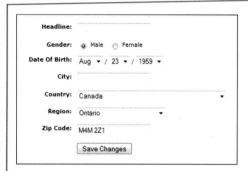

Fill In Your Profile

Once your MySpace account is active, log in using your e-mail address and password, and then click **Edit Profile**. MySpace divides your profile into several sections, including Interests, Name, Basic Info, and Details. For each section, click the section tab to open it, enter as much information as you feel comfortable sharing, and then click **Save Changes**.

Make Friends

Like any social networking site, MySpace is all about making friends, so the site gives you a number of ways to add friends to your profile. Position the mouse over the **Friends** tab and then click **Find Friends**. From here, you can search for people you know or look for people with common interests. If you find someone you know, display his or her profile, click the **Add to Friends** link, and then click the **Add to Friends** button. The other person must then confirm you as a friend.

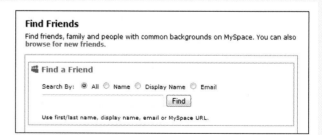

Add Content

You use MySpace by adding content to your profile, and your friends see this content when they visit your profile. Position the mouse ⌖ over the **Profile** tab, and then click the content you want. For example, click **My Photos** and then click **Upload Photos** to add one or more photos to your profile. You can also upload video files or record a video feed, and post to your MySpace blog.

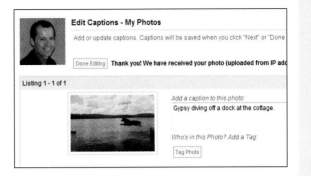

Contacting a Friend

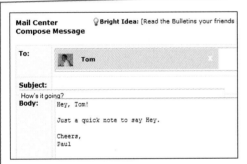

Your friends keep up with you by clicking your link in their Friend Space section to see your profile. You can also connect more directly with a friend. Display that friend's profile and then use the links in the Contacting *Friend* section (where *Friend* is the friend's display name). For example, click **Send Message** to send an e-mail message, or click **IM/Call** to send an instant message. You can also comment on a friend's photos, videos, and blog posts.

Work with Applications

MySpace comes with lots of built-in applications that you can add, and there are thousands of third-party applications for you to check out. Position the mouse ⌖ over **Profile**, click **My Apps**, and then click **Application Gallery**. Click a category and then click the application you want to add.

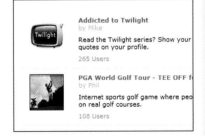

Change Settings

MySpace enables you to customize your account by offering dozens of settings. Click **My Account** to open the Settings page, which is divided into a number of categories, including Contact Info, Account, Password, and Privacy. Click the link you want, edit your account settings, and then click **Save Changes**.

Enhance Business Contacts with LinkedIn

LinkedIn (www.linkedin.com) is a social networking site that focuses on business contacts and professional networking. At the time of this writing, LinkedIn had more than 25 million users from 150 different industries. LinkedIn was founded in 2003.

Unlike other social networking sites, you do not add content to LinkedIn. Instead, you build a profile that contains your work and education history, skills, experience, interests, and other work-related data. You then establish contacts with people you know, and through those contacts you can find jobs, research companies, and find answers to questions.

Sign Up

Depending on the settings LinkedIn users have configured for their profile, nonmembers may see only a limited amount of data on a user's public profile. To see a user's full profile and to use the LinkedIn features, you must sign up for a LinkedIn account. To sign up, surf to the LinkedIn home page at www.linkedin.com and click the **Join Today** link.

Fill In Your Profile

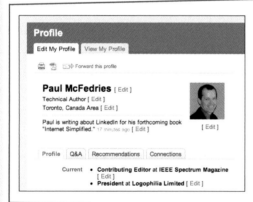

Once your LinkedIn account is active, log in using your e-mail address and password, and then click **Edit My Profile**. LinkedIn divides your profile into several sections, including Summary, Experience, Education, and Additional Information. For each section, click the **Edit** link, fill in the information requested, and then click **Save Changes**. Also, be sure to click **Edit Public Profile Settings** and then select the profile elements that you want nonmembers to see.

Make Connections

The main purpose of LinkedIn is to establish relationships with other members, who are called *connections*. LinkedIn gives you a number of ways to add connections to your profile. Click **Contacts** and then click **Add Connections**. In the Add Connections screen, you can invite people you know to join you on LinkedIn, import contacts from an online e-mail service or your computer's address book, or search for current or previous colleagues and classmates. In each case, the other person must confirm you as a connection.

Join a Group

LinkedIn comes with hundreds of groups that enable you to connect with people who share the same interests or careers. To join a group, click **Groups**, click the **Groups Directory** tab, type some text in the **Search Groups** box, and then click **Search**. If you see a group you would like to join, click the group's **Join this group** link, select the group options you prefer, and then click **Join this group**.

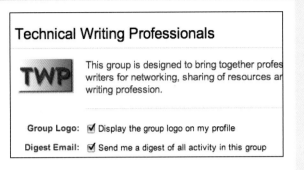

Find a Job

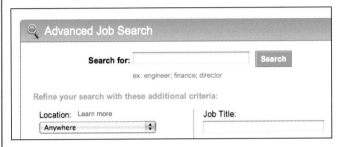

Many companies post jobs on LinkedIn, so you can use the site to find a job. Click **Jobs**, use the **Keywords** text box to type text that fits the type of job you want, select a country, and then click **Search**. For more control, click the **Advanced Job Search** tab, fill in criteria such as Location, Experience Level, and Job Function, and then click **Search**.

Find an Answer

With more than 25 million people on LinkedIn, you can be sure there are many people who are knowledgeable in just about any area of expertise you can think of. To take advantage of this, LinkedIn offers an Answers section where you can ask a question and other people on the site will provide you with answers. Click **Answers**, type your question in the **Ask a Question** text box, click **Next**, choose a category, and then click **Ask Question**.

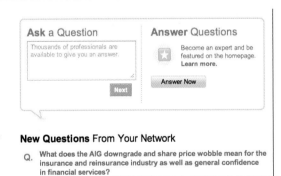

Research a Company

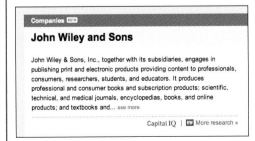

LinkedIn offers a large number of company profiles that enable you to research specific companies and connect with people who work at those companies. Click **Companies** and then either search for a specific company, or use the industry links to browse the available companies.

Explore Bebo

Bebo (www.bebo.com) is a popular social networking site with over 45 million users worldwide. Bebo started in early 2005 and was purchased by AOL in 2008.

Bebo enables you to build up a network of friends and then share content with those friends. For example, you can share photos and videos, you can exchange messages and drawings on your Bebo White Board, and you can post to your Bebo blog. There are also thousands of third-party applications that you can use to customize your Bebo experience.

Sign Up

Nonmembers can view features such as Bebo Video, Bebo Music, and Bebo Authors. However, you must be a Bebo member to view another member's profile. To sign up, surf to the Bebo home page at www.bebo.com and then click the **Sign Up** link.

Fill In Your Profile

Once your Bebo account is active, log in using your e-mail address and password, click **Profile**, and then click **Me, My Life, And I - Edit Now**. Bebo divides your profile into six sections: The Basics, Me, My Life, And I, These Are a Few of My Favorite Things, Public Profile Settings, IM Usernames, and My Contact Details. For each section, enter as much information as you feel comfortable sharing, and then click **Save**. Also, be sure to upload a profile photo. Click **Photos** and then click **Upload a Photo**.

Make Friends

Bebo gives you a number of ways to add friends to your profile. For example, you can search for people you know, or would like to know, view that person's profile, and then click **Add as Friend**. You can also click **Friends** and then click **Add Friends**. You can then use the Find Friends page to search your Gmail, Yahoo!, or Hotmail/MSN/Windows Live address book, or your AOL Instant Messenger buddies. The other person must then confirm you as a friend.

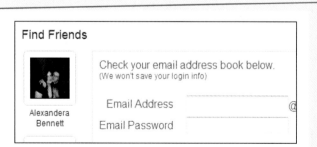

Add Content

You fill out your Bebo presence by adding content to your profile. Click **Profile**, and then click the tab of the type of content you want to add. For example, to upload a photo, click **Photos** and then click **Upload a Photo**, and to upload a video, click **Video** and then click **Upload a Video**. Note that in both cases you must install an add-on program to perform the upload. You can also click **White Board** to write or draw on your board, or **Blog** to add a post to your Bebo blog.

Work with Applications

You can extend Bebo by adding applications to your profile, and there are thousands of third-party applications for you to check out. Click **Explore** and then click **Apps** to open the Application Directory. Click a category, click an application and, if you like what you see, click **Try This App**.

Books

My Goodreads
By Otis Chandler

Goodreads is a place where you see what your friends a what you've read, list your favorite books, discuss literatu connect with other readers.

Avg. Rating:

add to my applications | details | rate it

Books iRead
By Krishna Motukuri, Mekin Maheshwari, Harish Abbott, Karthik Parinita, Ajit Pasi and John Smith

What you read says a lot about you! With iRead you can bookshelf. You can also rate and review books and read friends and other iReaders. iRead gives you exclusive b

Commercial Profiles

Bebo also allows commercial ventures to create their own profiles. For example, Bebo Video offers a number of channels from stations such as MTV and the BBC, as well TV shows, music videos, and more. Bebo Music offers profiles for singers, bands, and labels. Bebo Authors offers profiles for writers and books. Click **Explore** and then click **Video**, **Music**, or **Authors**.

Discover Other Social Networking Sites

Facebook, MySpace, LinkedIn, and Bebo are the most famous and the most popular of the social networking sites. However, there are dozens of other sites available, so if you prefer to go off the beaten track, you may find what you are looking for at one of the smaller sites.

For example, if you have a Google account, you might prefer to use Orkut since it is owned by Google. Similarly, if you are mostly into sharing media such as music and photos, you might find imeem more to your liking.

Ning

If no other social networking site is quite what you want, you can use Ning (www. ning.com) to create your own social network. You can configure your social network to accept various types of content, including photos, videos, chat, forums, groups, and blogs.

Ning

Sign Up or Sign In

Create Your Own Social Network

Name Your Social Network

For example, Paris Cyclists

Pick a Web Address

At least 6 letters. For example, pariscyclists.ning.com

Orkut

orkut beta

Connect with friends and family using scraps and instant messaging
Discover new people through friends of friends and communities
Share your videos, pictures, and passions all in one place

Orkut (www.orkut.com) is a social networking site that is owned by Google, and you access the site using your Google account. You can connect with friends by using your Scrapbook, an application that accepts short text- or HTML-based messages, which are called *scraps*. You can also upload photos or videos, create lists, and exchange messages. You can also augment your Orkut profile with third-party applications.

Jaiku

Jaiku (www.jaiku.com) is a social networking site that connects friends by means of short text messages called *jaikus*. You create an "activity stream" that includes jaikus and Web feeds, and those updates appear on the Updates section of each of your friends. Similarly, all your friends' posts appear in your Updates section.

imeem

imeem (www.imeem.com) is a special type of social networking site called a *social media service*. This means that imeem users interact mostly via media, including photos, videos, music, music videos, and music playlists. You establish connections with other imeem users based on your shared media tastes and interests.

Meetup

Meetup (www.meetup.com) is a social networking site that brings together people who have shared interests. However, instead of connecting with people online, as in most social networking sites, Meetup users get together offline in special *Meetup groups* such as book clubs, dinners, political rallies, and outdoor activities.

Classmates

Classmates (www.classmates.com) is a social networking site that enables you to connect with people you went to school with. You choose your school when you sign up, and Classmates shows you a list of every member who attended the same school. You can add classmates as friends, and then share messages, photos, and even organize reunions.

Learn About Social Networking Etiquette

To help make social networking a pleasant experience for you, for your friends and contacts, and for other users of the site, there are a few guidelines of social networking etiquette — sometimes called *netiquette*, a blend of *network* and *etiquette* — that you should know.

Note that these are guidelines, not rules. Social networking is still fairly new, so how people use these sites is still evolving. This means that not every idea in this section applies to every site or to every user of a site. If you are in doubt, be sure to ask your friends what they consider the correct course of action.

Adding Friends

One of the biggest conundrums on social networking sites is who you should add as friends. Your actual friends, family, and colleagues are fair game, of course, but what about acquaintances or even strangers? A good general rule is to not add friends just for the sake of padding the size of your friend list. Only add a friend if the two of you share a common interest, might do business together, or if that person comes recommended by another friend.

Personalize Friend Requests

When you send a friend request, most social networking sites include a generic text message. Whenever possible, you should edit that text message so that it is personalized for the person who is receiving the request. For friends and family, a simple greeting will do. For other people, you should include a short note reminding the person how you know each other or how you came across that person's profile.

Tailor Your Content

Whether you are adding text, photos, videos, or links to your social networking profile, be sure to tailor the content to the nature of the site. For example, LinkedIn is a business-oriented site, so you should avoid poor grammar, profanity, and risqué pictures. On a more relaxed site such as MySpace, a more casual approach to language and media is acceptable.

Do Not Abuse Information

Many people share a remarkable amount of information about their personal lives on their social network profiles. This information may include their home address, mobile phone number, and candid photos. Unless you know the person really well, do not attempt to contact someone other than through the normal site channels. Also, do not reproduce other peoples' photos or video elsewhere without permission.

Photos and Videos

Most social networking sites enable you to share photos and videos with your friends and, depending on your privacy settings, with friends of friends. Because this media could potentially be seen by dozens or even hundreds of people, do not post anything that would embarrass, denigrate, or ridicule another person.

Treat People with Respect

Always remember that the other people you deal with on a social networking site are human beings. Do not use your social networking profile to insult, badmouth, or humiliate other people, no matter how tempting (or deserved) it may be. If you do not want to be someone's friend, simply reject the request without explaining yourself. If another person adds negative comments to your profile, simply delete them and move on.

Avoid Facebook Pokes

When you view someone's Facebook profile, you can click the **Poke** link, and that person then sees the message **You were poked by** *Name*, where *Name* is your name. That person can then return the favor by clicking the **poke back** link. This is all harmless, of course, but not particularly useful. Many people get very annoyed by pokes, so you should keep them to a minimum.

Removing Friends

As in the offline world, online friendships can sometimes go sour. If you no longer want to have a connection with someone on a social networking site, it is okay to remove that person from your list of friends. However, it is always best to do this discreetly. That is, use the site's feature for removing friends, but do not augment the removal with a note or other message letting the person know that you have removed him. Note, too, that most sites do not announce when you have removed a friend.

Chapter 9

Buying and Selling Online

There are thousands of Web sites devoted to online shopping. Some sites focus on one product or service, such as books or travel, whereas other sites offer a wide range of goods and services. You can also find Web sites for traditional retailers such as Wal-Mart and Pottery Barn, and many manufacturers enable you to purchase goods directly through their Web sites.

The Web is also a great place to sell your goods and services. Auction sites enable people from anywhere in the world to bid for your goods. There are also several Web sites that enable you to set up a virtual store.

Understanding Online Commerce

E-commerce — the online buying and selling of goods and services — is a big part of the Web. You can use Web-based stores to purchase books, theater tickets, and even cars. Many sites also enable you to sell or auction your products or household items.

This section gives you an overview of the main aspects of e-commerce. In the sections that follow in this chapter, you will learn about each aspect in more detail.

Advantages

There are many advantages to e-commerce. For buying, you have the convenience of shopping at home, easily comparing prices and features, researching products, reading reviews from other users, and the ease of having goods delivered to your door. For selling, the Web offers low overhead, free or low-cost marketing opportunities, and a potential audience of millions of people.

Shopping Cart

When you shop at an e-commerce site, you usually add the items that you want to purchase to a virtual *shopping cart* — also called a *shopping basket* — that keeps track of these items and the quantity. Most sites have a View Cart link that enables you to view the contents of your shopping cart. The cart usually has a Proceed to Checkout link that leads you to a page where you provide your address and payment information.

Site Security

Purchasing anything on the Web requires that you provide accurate payment data, such as your credit card number and expiry date. To ensure that this sensitive data does not fall into the wrong hands, provide this payment data only on a secure site. Your browser may tell you when you are entering a secure site. Otherwise, look for "https" instead of "http" in the site address, and look for a lock icon in the browser window.

Buying and Selling Online

CHAPTER
9

Comparison Shopping

In the offline world, you comparison shop by visiting several stores that offer the same or similar goods or services, which can be time-consuming. In the online world, by contrast, comparing prices or features takes just a few mouse clicks. Even easier, sites such as PriceGrabber (www.pricegrabber.com) and ShopZilla (www.shopzilla.com) do the hard work for you by bringing together the online listings for a particular product.

Product Reviews

If you plan to make a purchase, whether it is a computer, a car, or a vacation, you can use the Web to research the product beforehand. There are sites devoted to product reviews by consumers, such as Epinions (www.epinions.com); reviews by companies, such as the J.D. Power Consumer Center (www.jdpower.com); and government resources, such as the Federal Citizen Information Center (www.pueblo.gsa.gov).

Online Auction

If you make your own products or have household items that you no longer need, you can put them up for sale in an online auction. By far, the most popular general online auction site is eBay (www.ebay.com), but there are also thousands of auction sites devoted to specific items, such as cars or memorabilia. Many auction sellers accept payment through the PayPal service (www.paypal.com), which transfers buyer credit card payments to your bank account.

Virtual Store

Many Web companies offer *e-commerce hosting* to enable you to set up your own online store. Sites such as Yahoo! Small Business (smallbusiness.yahoo.com) and FreeMerchant (www.freemerchant.com) offer tools, storage space, and expertise to build and promote your store. You can also use an online classifieds site such as craigslist (www.craigslist.org) to post ads for your goods.

Using the Web for Comparison Shopping

If you know exactly what you want to purchase online, you should take a bit of extra time to find the best price. Fortunately, plenty of sites on the Web can help you do this. These are the Web's price comparison sites — sometimes called *shopping portals* — where you select or specify the product you want and the site returns the product listings from a number of online retailers. You can then compare prices with just a few mouse clicks.

A number of sites on the Web also enable you to compare retailers by viewing user ratings and other data.

Compare Prices

Google Product Search

Google Product Search (formerly known as Froogle) applies the amazing power of Google's search engine to online products. You search on the name of the product you want, and Google returns product listings from around the Web. See www.google.com/products.

PriceGrabber

PriceGrabber is one of the most popular shopping portals. This is not surprising because for each product you get a great deal of information, including price, stock level, product details, user reviews and discussions, expert reviews, seller rating, and taxes and shipping for your ZIP code. In short, PriceGrabber gives you everything you need to make smart buying decisions. See www.pricegrabber.com.

ShopZilla

The ShopZilla site does not have all the bells and whistles that you see with some of the other sites, but it often returns a broader array of listings and has all the basic information you need: price, taxes, shipping, product details, and product reviews. See www.shopzilla.com.

Yahoo! Shopping

Lots of people like this section of Yahoo! because it provides all the standard shopping portal data and gives you full product specifications, user ratings, and the ability to send listings to a mobile phone (perfect if you do your shopping offline). See shopping.yahoo.com.

Compare Retailers

Ask Friends

With hundreds of online retailers out there, how can you tell which sites are legitimate and which ones are fly-by-night operations? The best way is to ask your friends, family, and colleagues who they have used and had good experiences with in the past. Because these are people you trust, you can rely on the information you get.

Retailer Ratings

You can also go by the ratings online users have applied to retailers. These are usually stars (usually up to 5 stars, and the more stars the better). Many of the shopping portals also include user ratings for each store. For example, Google Product Search (www. google.com/products) also doubles as a retailer ratings service. When you run a product search, the name of the reseller appears below the price and below that are a rating (1 to 5 stars) and the number of user ratings that have produced the result.

ResellerRatings.com

A site dedicated to rating resellers is the appropriately named ResellerRatings.com (see www.resellerratings.com). This site uses a 1-to-10 scale, where the higher the rating, the better the store.

Research Your Purchase Online

Whether you are looking for a car or a coffeepot, a big-screen TV or a bicycle, it is almost a certainty that someone has reviewed it and posted that review online for all to read. You can find many of these reviews on blogs and personal pages, and some of those are quite useful.

However, your product research time is most often better spent on sites that specialize in that kind of thing. Fortunately, the Web has plenty of places that offer in-depth, unbiased reviews by professionals that really put products to the test and tell you the pros and the cons of each item.

Product Information

Your online pre-purchase research should begin with gathering as much information as you can about the product you want to buy. Begin at the manufacturer's Web site and look for a product brochure, feature list, specifications, frequently asked questions (FAQ) list, and the product manual. Retailer sites should also provide product data.

Retailer Reviews

Many online retailers — particularly Amazon.com — solicit reviews from people who have purchased a product. This is a good idea because the product's merits and flaws are fresh in the mind of new purchasers. However, these reviews tend to vary widely in quality, so take them with a grain of salt. In general, it is best to give more weight to reviews that are more in-depth and that list specific pros and cons, and less weight to reviews that offer only vague opinions and sweeping generalizations.

Search for Reviews

Most mainstream products will have at least a few reviews online, and many have dozens. To help you locate these reviews, use a search engine such as Google (www.google.com) to search for the full product name, in quotation marks, followed by the word **review**, as in this example:

"Weber Genesis E-320" review

Consumer Reviews

The Web is home to many sites that consolidate product reviews by consumers. Some of the best sites are Epinions (www.epinions.com), ConsumerReview (www.consumerreview.com), ConsumerSearch (www.consumersearch.com), Review Centre (www.reviewcentre.com), Wize (www.wize.com), and Shopping.com (www.shopping.com).

Professional Reviews

There are a number of companies that specialize in reviewing products, and they all have Web sites that you can browse and search. See for example the J.D. Power Consumer Center (www.jdpower.com), Consumer Reports (www.consumerreports.org), Reviewboard Magazine (www.reviewboard.com), ConsumerGuide (www.consumerguide.com), and InfoFAQ (www.infofaq.com).

Government Resources

There are many government resources for consumers on the Web. In the United States, see Consumer.gov (www.consumer.gov), the Federal Citizen Information Center (www.pueblo.gsa.gov), and the Consumer Product and Safety Commission (www.cpsc.gov). In Canada, see Canadian Consumer Information (www.consumerinformation.ca), and in Britain see Consumer Direct (www.consumerdirect.gov.uk). Internationally, see Consumers International (www.consumersinternational.org).

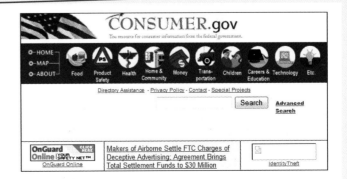

Make an Online Purchase

Once you have researched your product, read the reviews, and found the best price, you are ready to purchase the product.

Before beginning, make sure you have all the information you require. Typically, you need your full address, including your ZIP or postal code, your phone number, and your credit card number, expiration date, and security code.

Many retailers require you to have an account, so before making a purchase you should set up your account and then log in to the site.

This section uses Amazon.com for an example purchase. Other retailers use similar methods, although the procedure varies from site to site.

Make an Online Purchase

1. Locate the item you want to purchase.

2. Set the quantity.

3. Click **Add to Shopping Cart**.

   *Note: On some sites, you click **Add to Cart** or **Buy**.*

4. Repeat steps **1** to **3** to add more items.

5. Click **Cart**.

   *Note: On some sites, you click **View Cart** or **Shopping Cart**.*

   The site displays your selected items.

6. Adjust the item quantities, if necessary.

7. Delete any items you do not want.

8. Update the shopping cart if you made any changes.

9. Click **Proceed to Checkout**.

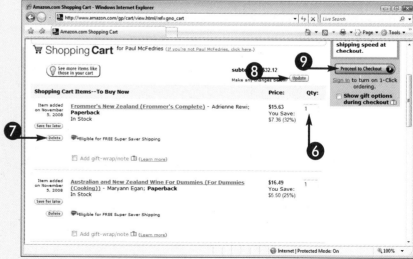

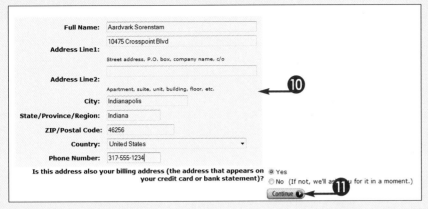

The site prompts you for your shipping and billing address.

⑩ Use the fields provided to type your address.

⑪ Click **Continue**.

Note: At this point Amazon asks for your shipping preferences, but I will skip this part here.

The site prompts you for your payment method.

⑫ Select the payment type (◎ changes to ◉).

⑬ Fill in the payment details, such as your credit card data.

⑭ Click **Continue**.

The site displays the order details.

⑮ Click **Place your order**.

The site submits your order and processes your payment.

How do PayPal purchases work?
If an online retailer supports PayPal, you will see some kind of PayPal button at the payment portion of the checkout. Clicking that button takes you to the PayPal site, where you log on using your PayPal account information. PayPal shows you the purchase details from the online retailer. You then process the payment through your PayPal account. Once the payment goes through, PayPal returns you to the online retailer's site, and you usually see your invoice or receipt.

How do online auctions work?
To use an auction site such as eBay (www.ebay.com) or Yahoo! Auctions (www.auctions.yahoo.com), you must first set up an account and then log on to the site. Locate the item you want, examine the previous bids, if any, and check the minimum bid. If you want the item, enter a bid equal to or greater than the minimum. Watch the item over the course of the auction. You may need to enter another bid if someone outbids you. If you win the auction, you receive an e-mail message that tells you how to purchase and receive the item.

Shop Online Securely

Shopping for things online is no longer the somewhat scary proposition that it was just a few years ago. There are now many reliable, reputable, and secure merchants to choose from, so buying online is a safe alternative to shopping offline.

However, buying from an online store is definitely different from buying at a retail store or via mail order. To ensure the most secure online transaction possible, there are a few pointers you need to bear in mind, as you see in this section.

Security Concerns

When you purchase goods or services online, the vendor asks you to provide accurate payment data. This almost always means typing your credit card number, the card's expiry date, and often the card's security code, along with your name and address. It is vital that this sensitive data does not fall into the wrong hands, so you need to ensure that you provide this payment data only on a secure site and that you follow other security precautions, as described in this section.

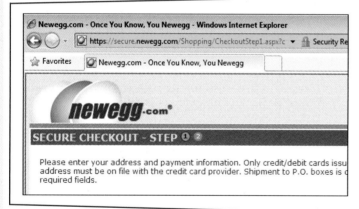

Security Indicators

To ensure that you are entering your confidential data on a secure site, the Web site and your Web browser display various indicators. On the site, look for "https" instead of "http" in the site address, and look for a security icon, such as "VeriSign Secured." In the Web browser, look for a lock icon somewhere in the browser window. If you are using Internet Explorer 7, the address bar shows a green background for a secure site.

Do Not Save Data

When you make a purchase online, many vendors offer to store your credit card information with your account (●). This is tempting because it saves you time on future orders if you do not have to locate and enter your credit card data the next time you shop at that store. However, this is a dangerous practice. For example, if a malicious hacker breaks into the retailer's network, he could steal your credit card data. Similarly, if you log in to the retailer's site and then leave your desk, someone could access your computer, purchase an item, and have it sent to an alternate address.

Avoid Checks

Some retailers allow you to mail a check or money order and will ship the order when they receive the payment. You should avoid these payment options because, if something goes wrong (for example, the product never shows up), getting your money back could be a challenge. If you pay by credit card, however, you always have the option of charging back the cost to the vendor.

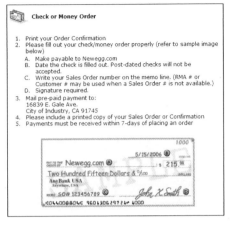

📁 **Check or Money Order**

1. Print your Order Confirmation
2. Please fill out your check/money order properly (refer to sample image below)
   A. Make payable to Newegg.com
   B. Date the check is filled out. Post-dated checks will not be accepted.
   C. Write your Sales Order number on the memo line. (RMA # or Customer # may be used when a Sales Order # is not available.)
   D. Signature required.
3. Mail pre-paid payment to:
   16839 E. Gale Ave.
   City of Industry, CA 91745
4. Please include a printed copy of your Sales Order or Confirmation
5. Payments must be received within 7-days of placing an order

1000
5/15/2006
Newegg.com $ 215.⁰⁰
Two Hundred Fifteen Dollars & ⁰⁰⁄₁₀₀
Any Bank USA
Anywhere, USA
MEMO SO# 123456789   John X Smith

Use PayPal

If the retailer offers a PayPal option, use it. Currently owned by eBay, PayPal is an online payment service that enables you to buy online without exposing your credit card data to the retailer. You sign up for a PayPal account at www.paypal.com and provide them with your credit card, debit card, or bank account information. When you buy something online with a PayPal-friendly retailer, that retailer tells PayPal the cost of the sale and PayPal charges it to your credit card, debit card, or bank account and then passes along the money to the retailer.

Extra Fees

Watch out for online retailers who charge some kind of extra fee (usually a percentage of the product price) for accepting credit card payments. This is almost always a sign of a shady dealer who is either trying to squeeze an extra few percentage points out of you or is trying to discourage you from using a credit card. Before completing the transaction, examine the details to make sure there are no other incidental fees.

	Price
Printer - Retail	~~$229.99~~ $169.99
Limited 30-Day Return Policy	
	$56.65
Subtotal	$169.99
Tax ⑦	$0.00
Shipping	$56.65
Order Total	$226.64

Check Postage

Most good online vendors give you a chance during checkout to enter your ZIP code or postal code so you can see exactly what your shipping charges will be. Because the cost of shipping can often be extravagant (●), whenever possible you should find out the cost in advance before completing the sale. Also, if you make a purchase on eBay, double-check the shipping charges because some unscrupulous sellers use them to hide extra profit.

Sell Your Goods and Services Online

Most people use the Web as a convenient way to purchase goods and services, but an increasing number of people are using the same convenience to sell products over the Web.

The Web offers several different methods for selling goods online, including auctions, classified ads, and joining an existing retail operation.

There are also sites that enable you to set up your own virtual store. Finally, if you have your own Web site, you may be able to configure it to sell your goods and services directly.

Auctions

If you are not sure what price to charge, or if you think you have a popular product, then you might want to sell your product using an online auction. In most cases, you are charged one fee for listing the item and another fee when you sell the item. The most popular online auction site is eBay (www.ebay.com), but you might also want to search for sites that specialize in auctioning the type of product you hope to sell.

Classifieds

If you know the price you want to charge for an item and you prefer to sell that item locally, then you should consider taking out an ad with an online classifieds site. Your local newspaper might have online classifieds, but most people use the local version of craigslist (www.craigslist.org). Another popular classifieds site is Kijiji (www.kijiji.com).

Online Retailer

Another common way to sell your goods is to sign up with an existing online retailer. This means your goods list along with the retailer's regular stock, and people can purchase your products exactly as they purchase the retailer's. The only difference is that you pack and ship the order. The biggest online retailer that offers this service is Amazon (see www.amazon.com/gp/seller/sell-your-stuff.html).

Set Up a Virtual Store

What to Look For

There are many businesses on the Web that enable you to set up a virtual store online. This is convenient because you do not have to worry about things like shopping carts, payment authorization, and security. When looking for a site, check the fees charged for setup and for each transaction. Also, be sure you know the store limitations, such as the number of products you can list and whether you must be a resident of a particular country. Make sure the site offers a secure shopping cart and credit card transactions.

Virtual Store Sites

Here are some sites that offer virtual storefronts:

Amazon (webstore.amazon.com)

CafePress (www.cafepress.com)

eBay (stores.ebay.com/)

Etsy (www.etsy.com)

HostWay (www.hostway.com/ecommerce)

SiteGround (www.siteground.com)

Yahoo! Small Business (smallbusiness.yahoo.com/ecommerce)

Sell on Your Site

E-commerce Needs

If you want to sell goods directly from your Web site, first check with your Web hosting provider to see if they offer an e-commerce package you can add to your site. If not, you will need to locate a shopping cart system that works with your site. You will also need to create Web pages for each of your products or services.

Payment Processing

When customers purchase from you, you need some way of obtaining the payment. The simplest method is to contact the customer and ask him or her to send you a check or money order for the full amount. A much more convenient method is to use a third-party payment service such as PayPal (www.paypal.com) or Google Checkout (checkout.google.com/sell/), which arranges a cash transfer from the customer's account to yours.

Chapter 10

Communicating via E-mail

You can use the Internet's e-mail system to send messages to and read messages from friends, family, colleagues, and even total strangers almost anywhere in the world. E-mail is one of the Internet's most popular services, with over 200 billion messages exchanged every day.

In this chapter you learn how e-mail works, and you learn how to compose a message, receive messages sent to you, reply to received messages, and practice good e-mail etiquette. You also learn how to subscribe to and use Internet mailing lists.

Introducing E-mail

E-mail is the Internet system that enables you to electronically exchange messages with other Internet users, wherever they may be. Almost anyone who has an Internet account also has access to e-mail, so theoretically you can communicate with almost any Internet user in the world. This versatility has made e-mail one of the most popular Internet services.

To help you get started with e-mail and to get more out of it, this section gives you some background about the system. You learn what advantages e-mail brings, what an e-mail account is, how the e-mail system works, and you get a tour of a typical e-mail program.

E-mail Advantages

The e-mail system is nearly universal because anyone who can access the Internet has an e-mail address. E-mail is fast because messages are generally delivered within a few minutes — sometimes a few seconds — after being sent. E-mail is convenient because you can send messages at any time of day, and your recipient does not need to be at his or her computer, or even connected to the Internet.

E-mail is inexpensive because you do not have to pay to send messages, no matter where in the world you send them. E-mail can also save you money because you can send a message instead of placing a long-distance phone call.

E-mail Account

To use e-mail, you must have an e-mail account, which is usually supplied by your Internet service provider (ISP). The account gives you an e-mail address to which others can send messages. See the section "Discover E-mail Addresses" for more information.

You can also set up Web-based e-mail accounts with services such as Hotmail.com and Yahoo.com. A Web-based account is convenient because it enables you to send and receive messages from any computer.

How E-mail Works

When you send an e-mail message, it travels along your Internet connection and then through your ISP's *outgoing mail server*. (This is also called an *SMTP server*, where SMTP stands for Simple Mail Transfer Protocol, the system that sends messages over the Internet.)

This server routes the messages to the recipient's *incoming mail server* (also often called a *POP server*, where POP stands for Post Office Protocol), which then stores the message in his or her mailbox. The next time the recipient checks for messages, your message is moved from the recipient's server to the recipient's computer.

E-mail Program

You can use an e-mail program to send and receive e-mail messages. Popular programs include Windows Mail (in Windows Vista), Outlook Express (in Windows XP), Mail (in Mac OS X), and Outlook (in Microsoft Office).

Folders

This area lists the program's folders, where it stores various types of messages:

- Inbox stores your incoming messages.
- Outbox stores outgoing messages that you have not yet sent.
- Sent Items stores outgoing messages that you have sent.

- Deleted Items stores messages that you have deleted from another folder.
- Drafts stores messages that you saved but have not yet finished composing.

- Junk E-mail stores messages that the e-mail program considers to be unsolicited commercial mail.

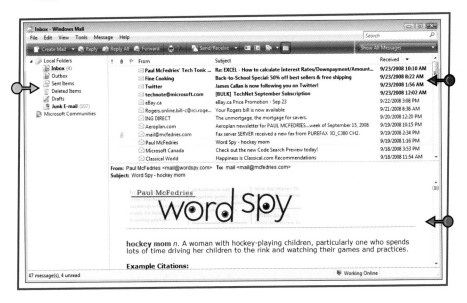

Messages

This area shows a list of the messages that are contained in the current folder.

Message Preview

This area shows a preview of the currently selected message.

Discover E-mail Addresses

Every e-mail account comes with its own e-mail address. An e-mail address is a set of characters that uniquely identifies the location of your Internet mailbox. The uniqueness of the address means that a message sent only to your address is delivered only to you and no one else.

When you send an e-mail message to another person, you must specify that person's e-mail address when you compose the message. This means that you can send an e-mail message to someone else only if you know his or her e-mail address.

Parts of an E-mail Address

User Name

The user name is the name of the person's account with the ISP or within his or her organization. This is often the person's first name, last name, or a combination of the two, but it could also be a nickname or some other text. No two people using the same ISP or within the same organization can have the same user name.

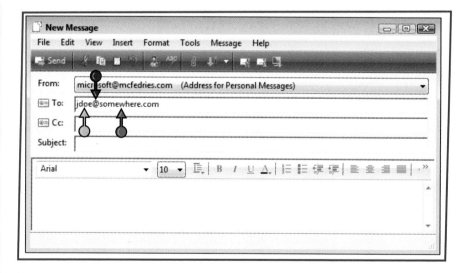

@ Symbol

The @ (pronounced "at") symbol separates the user name from the domain name in an e-mail address.

Domain Name

The domain name is the Internet name of the company that provides the person's e-mail account. This is usually the domain name of the ISP, an organization, or a Web e-mail service.

Multiple E-mail Addresses

Most ISPs provide their customers with multiple mailboxes, each of which has its own e-mail address. This is useful if you want to provide separate addresses for each member of your family or business. You can also use multiple addresses yourself. For example, you could use one for personal e-mail and another for mailing lists.

Address Book

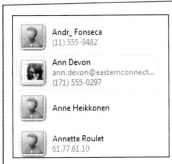

You can use your e-mail program's address book to store the names and addresses of people with whom you frequently correspond. When you compose a message, you can then choose the recipient's name from the address book, and the program automatically adds the contact's e-mail address. This is both faster and more accurate than typing the address manually.

Invalid Address

If you make an error in the recipient's address and then send it, your message cannot be delivered. If you type a nonexistent domain name, your e-mail program will likely display an error message, such as "Unable to resolve domain name," when you try to send the message. If you type the wrong user name, the message will go out, but you may receive a *bounce message* in return. Bounce messages report delivery errors. For an invalid user name, you may receive a "User unknown" or "Invalid recipient" error message (●).

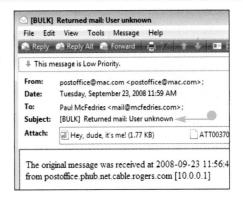

Search for an E-mail Address

You can use one of the Internet's *directory services* to find a person's e-mail address. A directory service such as Yahoo! People Search (people.yahoo.com) is a kind of Internet white pages that enables you to look up an e-mail address when you know the person's first and last name.

Compose and Send an E-mail Message

If you know the e-mail address of a person or organization, you can send an e-mail message to that address. In most cases, the message is delivered within a few minutes.

If you do not know any e-mail addresses, or, if at first, you prefer to just practice sending messages, you can send messages to your own e-mail address.

Compose and Send an E-mail Message

SEND A MESSAGE USING WINDOWS MAIL

① Click **Create Mail**.

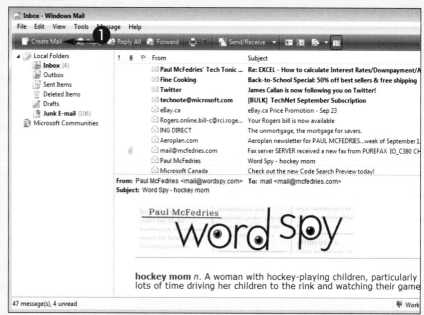

A message window appears.

② Type the e-mail address of the recipient.

③ Type a title or short description for the message.

④ Type the message.

⑤ Use the Formatting bar to format the message text.

⑥ Click **Send**.

Windows Mail sends your message.

Note: *Windows Mail stores a copy of your message in the Sent Items folder.*

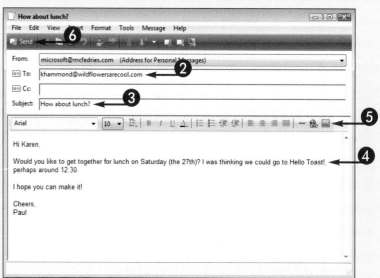

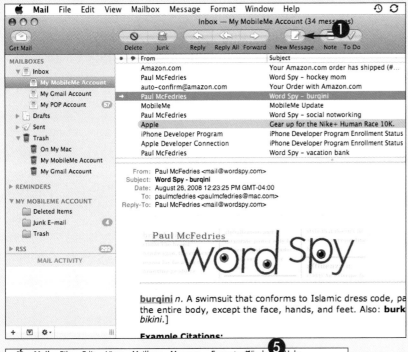

SEND A MESSAGE USING MAC OS X MAIL

1 Click **New Message**.

A message window appears.

2 Type the e-mail address of the recipient.

3 Type a title or short description for the message.

4 Type the message.

5 Use the Format menu to format the message text.

6 Click **Send**.

Mac OS X Mail sends your message.

Note: *Mail stores a copy of your message in the Sent folder.*

Simplify It

What is the Cc field for?
You use the Cc field to send a *courtesy copy*, which is a copy of a message that you send to one or more people as a courtesy so that these people are aware of the contents of your message. In your e-mail program, you specify the main recipients in the To field and the courtesy copy recipients in the Cc field. You can add multiple e-mail addresses in both the To line and the Cc line. Separate each address with a semicolon (;).

What writing style should I use in my messages?
In general, e-mail is more relaxed than formal writing, although messages to friends and family are more casual than business correspondence. Most of the time, e-mail contains short, to-the-point messages. This is particularly true in business, where most people use e-mail extensively. Therefore, being concise saves you time when composing a message, and it saves your recipient time when reading the message.

Attach a File to a Message

If you have a memo, an image, or another document that you want to send to another person, you can attach the file to an e-mail message.

Most e-mail messages consist only of text. However, you may often have other types of information to share. This could be a photo, a spreadsheet file, a word processing document, and any data that resides in a separate file.

When you attach the file and send the message, the file is sent along with the e-mail. The other person can then open the file after receiving your message.

Attach a File to a Message

ATTACH A FILE USING WINDOWS MAIL

1 Start a new message.

2 Click **Insert**.

3 Click **File Attachment**.

You can also click the **Attach File to Message** button (■).

The Open dialog box appears.

4 Click the file you want to attach.

5 Click **Open**.

● Windows Mail attaches the file to the message.

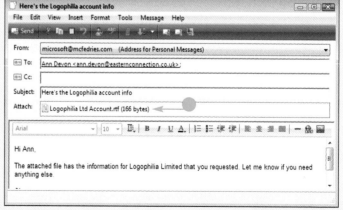

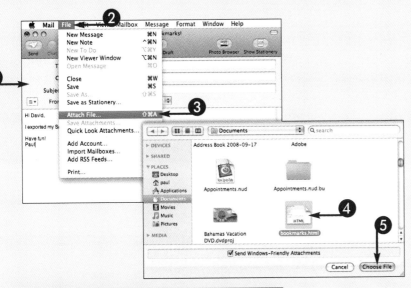

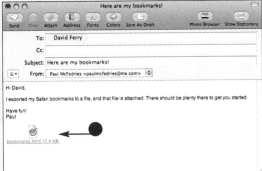

ATTACH A FILE USING MAC OS X MAIL

1 Start a new message.

2 Click **File**.

3 Click **Attach File**.

You can also click the **Attach** button (📎).

A Finder dialog box appears.

4 Click the file you want to attach.

5 Click **Choose File**.

● Mac OS X Mail attaches the file to the message.

Is there a limit to the number of files I can attach to a message?

There is no practical limit to the number of files you can attach to the message. However, you should be careful with the total *size* of the files you send. If you or the recipient has a slow Internet connection, sending or receiving the message can take an extremely long time. Also, many ISPs place a limit on the size of a message's attachments, which is usually around 2MB, but is often higher. In general, use e-mail to send only a few small files at a time.

Are there any restrictions on the types of files I can send?

Yes, most e-mail programs block access to file types that could harbor a computer virus or other malicious data. These file types include programs, scripts, and batch files. In most cases, if you attempt to send a potentially restricted file, your e-mail program will warn you that your recipient might not be able to open the file.

Receive E-mail Messages

A message sent to you by another person is stored on your ISP's incoming e-mail server. You must connect to the ISP's server to retrieve and read the message.

All e-mail programs have a command that you can run to check for new messages on your ISP's incoming mail server. Make sure that you are connected to the Internet before you run this command.

In addition, most e-mail programs automatically check the incoming mail server for new messages. For example, Windows Mail automatically checks for new messages every 30 minutes, and Mac OS X Mail automatically checks for new messages every 5 minutes.

Receive E-mail Messages

RECEIVE MESSAGES USING WINDOWS MAIL

① Click **Send/Receive**.

Windows Mail checks the server for new messages.

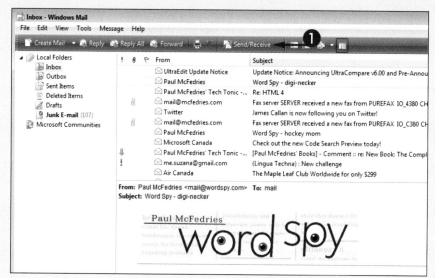

● New messages appear in your Inbox folder in bold type.

● The symbol 📎 means the message has a file attached.

● The symbol ❗ means the message has high priority.

● The symbol ⬇ means the message has low priority.

② Click the message.

● The message appears in the preview pane.

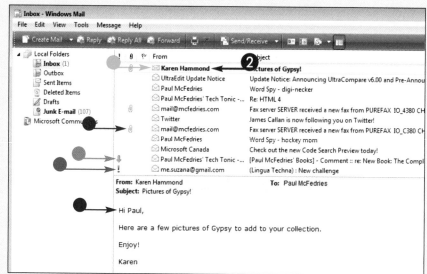

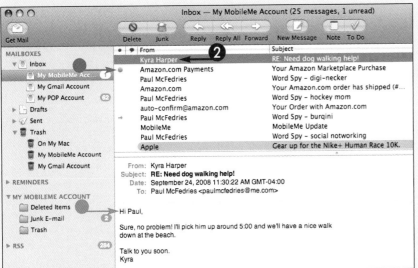

RECEIVE MESSAGES USING MAC OS X MAIL

1 Click **Get Mail**.

Mac OS X Mail checks the server for new messages.

New messages appear in your Inbox folder.

● The symbol ⊡ means the message is unread.

2 Click the message.

● The message appears in the preview pane.

Can I change how often my e-mail program checks for messages?
Yes. In Windows Mail, click **Tools**, click **Options**, and then click the **General** tab. Use the **Check for new messages every** text box to type a new time interval, in minutes, and then click **OK**. In Mac OS X Mail, click **Mail**, click **Preferences**, and then click the **General** tab. Click the **Check for new mail** ⬚, click the time interval you want to use, and then close the dialog box.

Can I stop my e-mail program from checking for messages automatically?
Yes. In Windows Mail, click **Tools**, click **Options**, and then click the **General** tab. Click the **Check for new messages every** check box (☑ changes to ☐), and then click **OK**. In Mac OS X Mail, click **Mail**, click **Preferences**, and then click the **General** tab. Click the **Check for new mail** ⬚, click **Manually**, and then close the dialog box.

Handle Message Attachments

If you receive a message that has a file attached to it, you need to know how to handle that attachment.

In this case, handling the attachment means doing one of two things: viewing the file or saving the file.

If you only want to take a brief look at an attached file, you can open it directly from the e-mail message, and then close the file when you are done.

If you would prefer to keep a copy of the attached file, you can save the file from the e-mail message to your computer's hard drive.

Handle Message Attachments

HANDLE ATTACHMENTS IN WINDOWS MAIL

1. Click the message that contains the attachment.

2. Click the **Attachment** icon (📎).

● If you only want to view a file, click it to open it.

3. To save the file, click **Save Attachments**.

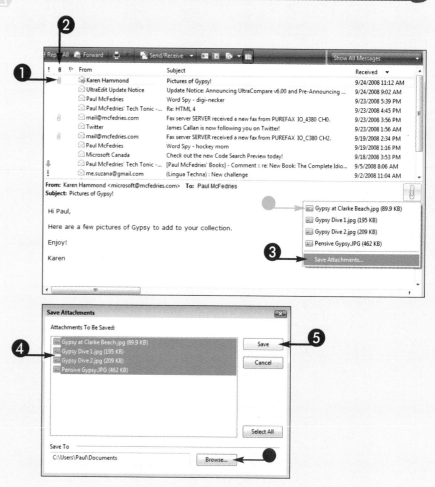

The Save Attachments dialog box appears.

4. Press and hold **Ctrl** and click each file you want to save.

● If you want to save the files to a different folder, click **Browse** and then choose the folder.

5. Click **Save**.

Windows Mail saves copies of the files to your hard drive.

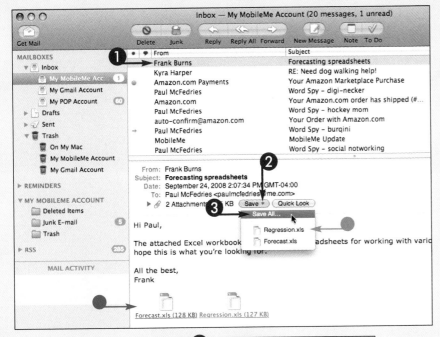

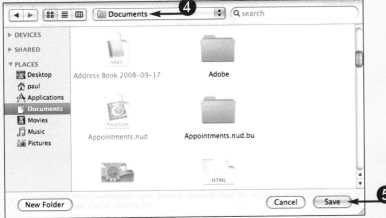

HANDLE ATTACHMENTS IN MAC OS X MAIL

1 Click the message that contains the attachment.

● If you only want to view a file, double-click it to open it.

2 To save the file, right-click (or `Ctrl` + click) **Save**.

3 Click **Save All**.

● If you just want to save a single file, click that file, instead.

A Finder dialog box appears.

4 Choose the folder where you want to save the files.

5 Click **Save**.

Mac OS X Mail saves copies of the files to your hard disk.

Why does my computer not open the file attachment?
Instead of opening the file, your computer may display a dialog box telling you that the file "does not have a program associated with it." This means you need to install the appropriate program for the type of file. If you are not sure, ask the person who sent you the file what program you need.

Why am I unable to click either the file name or the Save Attachments command?
Windows Mail has determined that the attached file may be unsafe, meaning that the file may harbor a virus or other malicious code. To confirm this, double-click the message to open it. Below the toolbar, you should see a message saying, "Windows Mail removed access to the following unsafe attachments in your mail." See Chapter 11 to learn more about e-mail security.

Reply to a Message

When a message you receive requires some kind of response, you can send a reply to the person who sent the message.

Some e-mail messages only supply you with information or data, and those types of messages generally do not require a response. However, you will receive many messages where the sender is expecting a reply from you.

You may need to answer a question, supply requested information, or provide comments or criticisms concerning some topic raised by the sender. In each case, you need to compose and send a reply to either the original sender or, in some cases, to all the recipients of the original message.

Reply to a Message

REPLY TO A MESSAGE WITH WINDOWS MAIL

① Click the message to which you want to reply.

② Click **Reply**.

● Click **Reply All**, instead, to respond to all the addresses in the To and Cc lines.

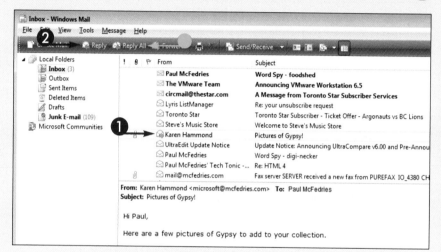

A message window appears.

● Windows Mail automatically inserts the sender.

● Windows Mail inserts the subject line, preceded by Re.

● Windows Mail includes the original message.

Note: *If the original message is long, edit the message to show only text that is relevant to your reply.*

③ Type your reply.

④ Click **Send**.

Windows Mail sends your reply.

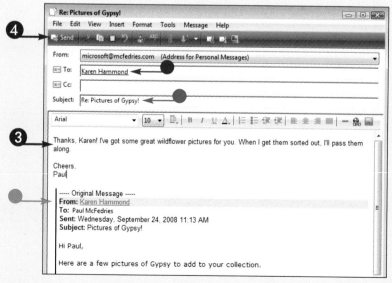

174

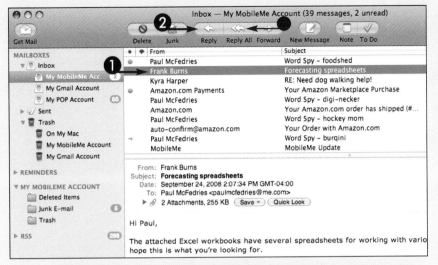

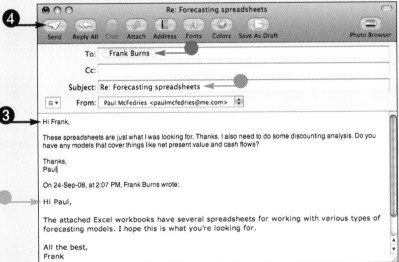

REPLY TO A MESSAGE WITH MAC OS X MAIL

1 Click the message to which you want to reply.

2 Click **Reply**.

● Click **Reply All**, instead, to respond to all the addresses in the To and Cc lines.

A message window appears.

● Mac OS X Mail automatically inserts the sender.

● Mac OS X Mail inserts the subject line, preceded by Re.

● Mac OS X Mail includes the original message.

Note: *If the original message is long, edit the message to show only text that is relevant to your reply.*

3 Type your reply.

4 Click **Send**.

Mac OS X Mail sends your reply.

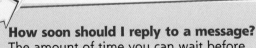

How soon should I reply to a message?
The amount of time you can wait before sending a reply depends on a number of factors. If the message is urgent or sent with high priority, you should answer as soon as you can. If the message is requesting information or data from you, wait until you have gathered the necessary material. If the message is not urgent or timely, there is no harm in waiting an hour or two before replying. However, you should always reply within 24 hours.

Each time I reply to a message, Windows Mail adds the recipient to my Contacts list. How do I stop this?
In Windows Mail, click **Tools** and then click **Options** to open the Options dialog box. Click the **Send** tab. Click the **Automatically put people I reply to in my Address Book** check box (☑ changes to ☐). Click **OK** to put the new setting into effect.

Forward a Message to Another Person

You can send another person a copy of a message that you have received. This is called *forwarding* the message, and the copy you send is called a *forward*.

You may receive a message that contains information that you think might be relevant or interesting to another person, or that contains information that concerns another person.

Whatever the reason, you can ensure that the other person sees the information by forwarding a copy of the message to that recipient.

Your e-mail program automatically adds "Fw" (or "Fwd") to the subject line to indicate a forward. You can also include your own comments in the forward.

Forward a Message to Another Person

FORWARD A MESSAGE WITH WINDOWS MAIL

① Click the message you want to forward.

② Click **Forward**.

A message window appears.

● Windows Mail inserts the subject line, preceded by Fw.

● Windows Mail shows the original message.

Note: *If the original message is long, edit the message to show only text that you want to forward.*

③ Type the e-mail address of the recipient.

④ Type your message.

⑤ Click **Send**.

Windows Mail forwards the message.

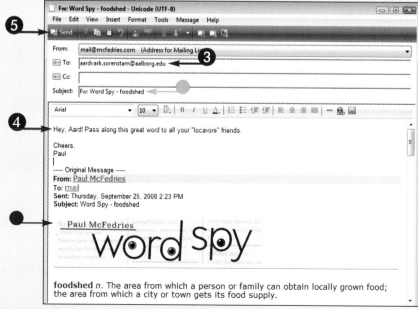

176

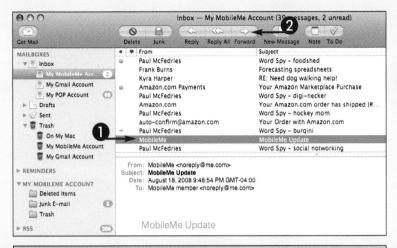

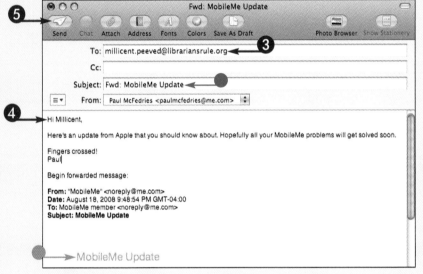

FORWARD A MESSAGE WITH MAC OS X MAIL

① Click the message you want to forward.

② Click **Forward**.

A message window appears.

● Mac OS X Mail inserts the subject line, preceded by Fwd.

● Mac OS X Mail shows the original message.

Note: If the original message is long, edit the message to show only text that you want to forward.

③ Type the e-mail address of the recipient.

④ Type your message.

⑤ Click **Send**.

Mac OS X Mail forwards the message.

Simplify It

How do I forward someone a copy of the actual message instead of just a copy of the message text?
You can send the original message as a separate attachment. This works the same in both Windows Mail and Mac OS X Mail. Click the message you want to forward, click the **Message** menu, and then click **Forward as Attachment**. The program creates a new message and includes the original message as an attachment. Address the message, type some text, and then click **Send**.

My replies and forwards do not always use the same format. How can I make my program use a single format?
In Windows Mail, click **Tools**, click **Options**, click the **Send** tab, click **Reply to messages using the format in which they were sent** (☐ changes to ☑), and then click either **HTML** or **Plain Text** (◉ changes to ◉). Click **OK**. In OS X Mail, click **Mail**, click **Preferences**, click **Composing**, click **Use the same message format as the original message** (☑ changes to ☐), and then click the **Message Format** you want to use.

Learn About E-mail Etiquette

To help make e-mail a pleasant experience for you and your correspondents, there are a few rules of e-mail etiquette — sometimes called *netiquette*, a blend of *network* and *etiquette* — that you should know.

Note, however, that e-mail netiquette is better described as a set of *guidelines*, not rules. That is because no one enforces e-mail netiquette. Instead, it is up to each e-mail user to understand and implement the guidelines as best as he or she can.

Do Not SHOUT

Use the normal rules of capitalization in your e-mail text. In particular, AVOID LENGTHY PASSAGES OR ENTIRE MESSAGES WRITTEN IN CAPITAL LETTERS, WHICH ARE DIFFICULT TO READ AND MAKE IT APPEAR THAT YOU ARE SHOUTING. It is okay to use capital letters occasionally to EMPHASIZE a single word.

Write Good Subjects

Busy e-mail readers often use a message's subject line to decide whether to read the message. This is particularly true if the recipient does not know you. Therefore, do not use subject lines that are either vague or overly general, such as "Info required" or "Message." Make your subject line descriptive enough so that the reader can tell at a glance what your message is about.

Quote Appropriately

When replying to a message, make sure that the other person knows what you are responding to by including quotes from the original message in your reply. Most e-mail programs quote all of the original message when you create a reply. However, quoting the entire message is usually wasteful, especially if the message is lengthy. Edit the quote to include enough of the original message to put your reply into context.

Do Not Request Read Receipts

Most e-mail programs have an option that enables you to request a *read receipt*. This is a message that the recipient's e-mail program sends back to you as soon as the recipient opens your message, and it is a way of knowing when the other person has read your message. Most people consider read receipts to be an invasion of privacy, so do not request them.

Get Permission

If you receive private e-mail correspondence from someone, it is considered impolite to quote the text of that message in another message or some other context, such as a World Wide Web page or blog post. If you want to use that person's words, you must write to him or her and ask for permission.

Reply Promptly

When you receive a message in which the sender expects a reply from you, it is considered impolite to wait too long before responding. Whenever possible, urgent or time-sensitive messages should be answered within a few minutes to an hour. For other correspondence, you should reply within 24 hours.

Be Patient

E-mail is fast, but it is not meant for instantaneous communications. See Chapter 12 for information related to instant messaging. If you send someone a message, do not expect an immediate response. Instead, expect the other person to take at least 24 hours to get back to you. If you have not heard back within 48 hours, it is okay to write a short note asking the person whether your message was received.

Do Not Send Flames

If you receive a message with what appears to be a thoughtless or insulting remark, your immediate reaction might be to compose an emotionally charged, scathing reply. Such a message is called a *flame*, and it will probably only make matters worse. Allow yourself at least 24 hours to cool down before responding to the message.

Subscribe to a Mailing List

A *mailing list* is a discussion group in which message are exchanged through e-mail. Most mailing lists are free, although some require a small subscription fee.

Most mailing lists deal with a particular subject, such as dogs or bread making. There are thousands of mailing lists available, covering virtually any topic that you can think of.

To receive messages from a mailing list, you must first subscribe to that list.

The majority of mailing lists allow any list subscriber to post messages, but some lists act more like newsletters, where a single person or organization sends periodic messages to the list subscribers.

How a Mailing List Works

Each mailing list has a *list owner*, which is the person or company that runs the mailing list. One of the list owner's duties includes maintaining the collection of subscribers, each of which is a person or organization that has provided the mailing list with an e-mail address. When the list owner or a subscriber sends a message to the mailing list, a copy of the message is sent to each subscriber.

Mailing List Moderator

Most mailing lists allow any subscriber to send messages to the list. This is not a problem most of the time, but some subscribers abuse the system by sending offensive, off-topic, or commercial messages to the list. If this happens too often, the mailing list may add a *moderator*, a person who examines each message before it is sent to the list. If the message is appropriate, the moderator forwards the messages to the list; if the message is inappropriate, the moderator deletes it.

Newsletters

Many mailing lists are *broadcast only*, meaning that only the list owner can send messages. These types of mailing lists are often called *newsletters*. An example is the Word Spy mailing list (see www.wordspy.com), a post to which is shown here. Many corporations and organizations have newsletters that you can sign up for.

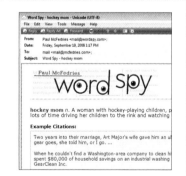

Search for a Mailing List

If you do not know of any mailing lists to join, there are mailing list directories on the Web. You can use these directories to search for a list that interests you. Two examples are Tile.Net (www.tile.net/lists) and CataList (www.lsoft.com/lists/listref.html). The information the directory provides gives you a description of the list and instructions for subscribing.

Subscribe

To receive messages from a mailing list and to post messages to the list (if allowed), you must first *subscribe* to the list, which means supplying the list owner with your e-mail address. For most lists, this means sending an e-mail message to the list's subscription address, sometimes with a command such as Subscribe in the subject line. However, many mailing lists also allow you to subscribe via the Web, as shown here.

1. Check your email address:
   mail@wordspy.com
   Get your updates via:
   - ✉ ⦿ Email
   - ⊗ ⦾ Skype
   - 🅰 ⦾ AOL Instant Messenger
   - ⤷ ⦾ Twitter (public, for your followers)
   - ⤵ ⦾ Microsoft Messenger
   - ⤷ ⦾ Twitter (private, direct to you only)
   - 🆈 ⦾ Yahoo! Messenger

Instructions

After your mailing list subscription is processed, the list owner usually sends you an e-mail message to confirm your subscription and to provide instructions for using the list. For example, the instructions will provide you with separate addresses for sending messages to the list and for sending administrative requests to the list owner. Always save these instructions for future use.

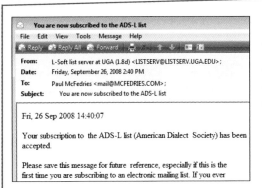

Digest Version

On a busy mailing list, you may find that you have dozens of messages arriving in your Inbox daily. If you find it time consuming to deal with so many individual messages, switch to the list's *digest* version, if it has one. A digest is a single e-mail that includes all of the messages sent during a particular time, such as a day or a week.

Vacation Stop

If you are going on vacation for a week or more, you may not want hundreds of mailing list messages waiting for you when you return. To prevent this, most lists allow you to temporarily stop your subscription for the duration of your vacation. If you cannot temporarily stop the list messages, consider unsubscribing from the list and then resubscribing when you return.

Learn About Mailing List Etiquette

Mailing list etiquette consists of a few simple rules that subscribers are encouraged to follow to ensure that the mailing list remains useful and sociable.

As with the e-mail etiquette discussed earlier in this chapter, mailing list etiquette is a set of guidelines that subscribers are expected to follow, but that are generally not enforced.

The only exception to this is with some moderated lists, where the moderator may enforce etiquette rules. For example, the moderator may delete any message that breaches list etiquette. If a subscriber repeatedly flouts list etiquette, the moderator may revoke that person's subscription.

Read Before Posting

A mailing list is an inherently social medium where the subscribers often come from a wide variety of backgrounds and exhibit a wide variety of personalities. When you first subscribe to a list, spend a week or two just reading the posts, a process called *lurking*. This gives you a feel for the conversation and helps you to avoid posting messages that are inappropriate.

Read the FAQ

Every mailing list has its own rules, methods, and quirks, and every mailing list topic has a few obvious questions that every beginner to the topic wants to ask. The list owner often takes these common items and combines them in a document called the Frequently Asked Questions list, or FAQ. After you subscribe to the list, and before you post any messages to the list, read the FAQ to find out more about the list and to learn the answers to the most common questions.

Stay On Topic

When you post a message to the list, be sure that the content of your message is related to the overall mailing list topic. For example, if the list topic is bread making, you can post messages about bread, flour, yeast, kneading, proofing, and bread recipes, but not about cars or movies or anything else that is not directly related to the making of bread.

Avoid Trivial Replies

Mailing lists are often quite busy, and many generate dozens of messages each day. Most mailing list subscribers understand this, and they appreciate the time that people take to craft thoughtful and informative posts. However, they do not appreciate having their mailboxes cluttered with trivial replies that add nothing to the conversation. Do not send posts where the content of your message is "Me too" or "Okay" or "Thanks."

Reply Privately

Most mailing lists display the e-mail address of the person who posts each message. If you have a response that is only of interest to the person who posted the message and not to the entire list, copy the sender's address and use it to send a reply just to that person.

Be sure to start a new message when you reply privately. If you simply run your e-mail program's Reply command, your response is usually sent to all of the list subscribers.

Do Not Send Attachments

Never attach a file to a message that you send to a mailing list without permission from the list owner. Most list subscribers do not want large attachments clogging their mailboxes, and so sending a large file to hundreds or thousands of people wastes bandwidth and can bog down the server that runs the mailing list. Attachments are such a problem that many mailing lists strip them out of messages automatically.

Chapter 11

Enhancing E-mail Security and Privacy

Although most e-mail messages are benign, many messages contain threats to your security and privacy. These threats include junk e-mail, viruses lurking in file attachments or message code, and messages that aim to trick you into revealing confidential or private data, such as passwords or credit card numbers.

To protect yourself and your family, you need to understand these threats and know what you can do to thwart them. This chapter introduces you to this negative side of the Internet's e-mail system and shows you specific steps you can take to keep your e-mail inbox secure and private.

Understanding Junk E-mail Messages

Junk e-mail — also called *spam* — refers to unsolicited, commercial e-mail messages that advertise a wide variety of products, from baldness cures to cheap printer cartridges.

Junk e-mail product pitches are frustrating to deal with because they clog up your mailbox and you have to waste time deleting.

However, some junk e-mail messages are more than just annoying. For example, many junk messages advertise deals that are simply fraudulent, some messages contain profanity or offensive images, and others feature such unsavory practices as linking to adult-oriented sites or to sites that install spyware.

Junk E-mail

Junk e-mail refers to any e-mail message of a commercial nature that is unsolicited. That is, if you never asked to receive messages from a company, or if you have had no commercial dealings with a company in the recent past, then any commercial messages you receive from that company are classified as junk e-mail. A person or organization that sends such messages is called a *junk e-mailer* or, more commonly, a *spammer*. In the United States, by law, unsolicited commercial e-mail must be labeled as such, although few spammers do this.

Non-Junk E-mail

If you receive an e-mail message for a product or service, that message is not necessarily junk e-mail. If you purchased a product recently, that company may simply be following up with your order. Similarly, if you opted to receive a newsletter or other communications from the company, then the messages are technically not junk e-mail because you asked to have them sent to you.

Junk E-mail Volume

The amount of junk e-mail sent each day is staggering and has been estimated to comprise between 80 and 90 percent of all daily e-mail traffic. This means that well over 100 billion junk e-mail messages are sent each day, and that number is still growing, although not as quickly as a few years ago when spam volume was roughly doubling each year.

Junk E-mail Filter

Of the billions of junk e-mail messages sent each day, only a small fraction are delivered successfully, mostly because spammer address lists contain many invalid addresses. However, many Internet service providers maintain special software called a *junk e-mail filter* that can detect spam and delete it before it gets delivered. Also, most e-mail programs — including Windows Mail, Microsoft Outlook, and Mac OS X Mail — come with built-in junk e-mail filters that catch most incoming spam.

Enhancing E-mail Security and Privacy

Types of Junk E-mail

Product Pitches

By far the most common type of junk e-mail message is a straightforward advertisement for a commercial product or service. According to spam experts, e-mail advertisements for products (such as fake high-end watches), financial services (particularly for getting out of debt), and health aids (Viagra and related treatments) account for nearly 60 percent of junk e-mail.

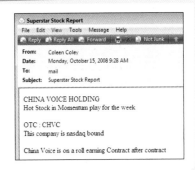

Offensive

Approximately 20 percent of all junk e-mail messages contain some kind of offensive content. This may include profanity, racist remarks, or other objectionable text. However, most offensive junk e-mail messages are related to adult-oriented Web sites. This means that the message may contain salacious images, or it may contain one or more links to sites that display such images.

Scams

Many junk e-mail messages are scams that advertise nonexistent products, services, and money-making opportunities. The most common of these is the so-called *advance fee fraud*, in which a person is asked for money to help secure the release of, and so earn a percentage of, a much larger sum. These scams often originate in Nigeria, so they are sometimes called *419 scams*, because 419 is the section number of the Nigerian penal code that covers this sort of fraudulent behavior.

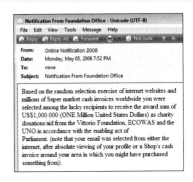

Viruses and Phishing

Many junk e-mail messages do not try to sell you anything at all. Instead, the spam message is really a vehicle for either a virus or a phishing attempt. A virus is a malicious program that attempts to take over or crash your computer; see "Guard Against E-mail Viruses" later in this chapter. A phishing message attempts to trick you into supplying confidential or sensitive data; see "Guard Against Phishing Attempts," later in this chapter.

Reduce Junk E-mail

The anti-spam filters Internet service providers employ capture a large percentage of the billions of junk e-mail messages sent each day. However, most people still receive at least a few spams a day, while some people receive hundreds of them.

No matter how many you receive, it takes time to ensure a message is junk and then delete that message. It is also quite frustrating to deal with spam, particularly the scams and offensive messages.

So it pays to take steps to reduce the number of junk e-mail messages that you receive. Reducing spam not only saves you time, but it also reduces e-mail frustration.

Do Not Open Spam

Never open suspected spam messages or display them in your e-mail program's preview pane. Doing so can sometimes notify the spammer that you have opened the message.

Notifying the spammer in this way is a big problem because it confirms that the message was delivered to you successfully. This proves to the spammer that your address is legitimate, and so you will likely receive even more spam.

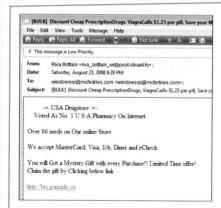

Do Not Respond to Spam

Never respond to spam, even to an address within the spam that claims to be a "removal" address. If you respond to the spam, all you are doing is proving that your address is legitimate.

Similarly, never click a Web site link that appears within a spam. At best, clicking the link may prove that your address is active. At worst, the link may take you to a site that displays objectionable content or that surreptitiously installs spyware on your computer.

Disable E-mail Images

A *Web bug* is an image embedded in a spam that downloads from the spammer's Web site, even if you simply preview the message. This tells the spammer that your address is active. Many e-mail programs enable you to disable e-mail images.

For example, in Windows Mail, click **Tools**, click **Options**, click the **Security** tab, and then select **Block images and other external content in HTML e-mail**. In Mac OS X Mail, click **Mail**, click **Preferences**, click the **Viewing** tab, and then select **Display remote images in HTML messages**.

Alter Your Newsgroup Address

The most common method that spammers use to gather addresses is to harvest them from newsgroup posts. Therefore, never use your actual e-mail address in a newsgroup account.

If you want other newsgroup users to be able to e-mail you, one common solution is to alter your newsgroup e-mail address by adding text that invalidates the address but is still obvious for other people to figure out. For example, if your real e-mail address is myname@myisp.com, then you could alter the address to myname@delete-this-to-e-mail-me-myisp.com.

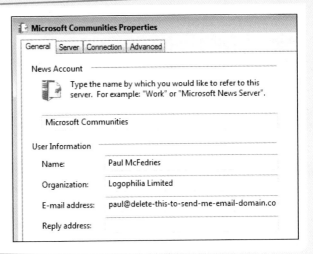

Use a Fake Web Address

When you sign up for something online, use a fake address if possible. If you must use your real address because you need or want to receive e-mail from the company, make sure that you deselect any options that ask whether you want to receive promotional offers.

Another solution is to supply the site with the address from a free Web-based account (such as a Windows Live Hotmail account), so that any spam that you receive is sent there instead of to your main address.

Anti-Spam Software

A number of companies offer anti-spam programs and services that do a good job of filtering out most junk e-mail. Some popular programs and services in this category are OnlyMyEmail (www.onlymyemail.com), iHateSpam (www.sunbeltsoftware.com), and Norton Internet Security (www.symantec.com).

Guard Against E-mail Viruses

A *virus* is a malicious software program usually designed to either crash your computer or damage your files. Most viruses propagate through e-mail in the form of file attachments. When you open the attachment, the virus infects your computer.

Large-scale virus outbreaks occur because some viruses surreptitiously use an infected computer's e-mail program to send out messages with more copies of the virus attached. These messages are usually sent to people in the computer's address book. Some of those recipients open the file and the virus spreads further.

You can take a few simple precautions to avoid virus infections.

Attachments from Strangers

There is no reason why a stranger should send you an attachment. Note, however, that the word "stranger" here does not include businesses and organizations that you have a relationship with, because those entities may send you things like invoices and newsletters as attachments. A stranger is a person, company, or organization that you do not know and that you have never had any dealings with in the past. If a stranger sends you a message that has an attachment, do not open the attachment.

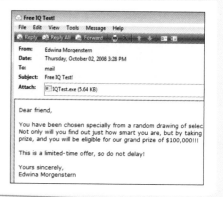

Attachments from Friends

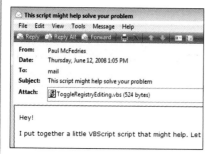

If a friend unexpectedly sends you a message with an attachment, do not assume that the attachment is benign. The friend's computer may be infected with a virus that e-mails copies of itself. Send a message to your friend to confirm that he or she actually sent the file. If you receive a message with an attachment from a company or organization that you deal with, the attachment is likely benign. However, examine the message carefully to ensure that it is not a fake.

Delete Virus Messages

If you receive a message with a file attachment that you suspect is a virus, delete the message immediately. Even if you are only slightly suspicious about a message, if you have no other way to verify that it is legitimate, delete the message anyway. In all cases it is better to permanently delete a message rather than send it to the Deleted Items folder. In Windows Mail, Outlook Express, and Microsoft Outlook, click the message, press **Shift** + **Delete**, and then click **Yes** when asked to confirm.

Read in Plain Text

The HTML message format uses the same codes that create Web pages. Therefore, just as some Web pages are unsafe, so are some e-mail messages. Those messages contain malicious scripts that run automatically when you open or even just preview the message.

You can prevent these scripts from running by changing your e-mail program settings to read all of your messages in the plain text format. You can do this in most e-mail programs, including Windows Mail, Outlook Express, and Microsoft Outlook.

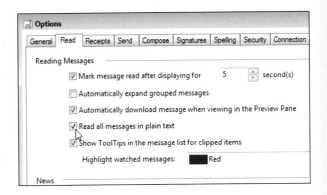

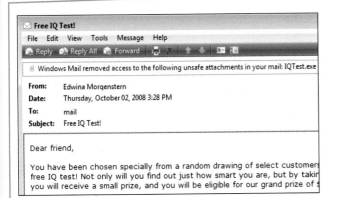

E-mail Program Security

Most e-mail programs offer security against viruses. For example, the program may come with a setting that prevents other programs from sending mail using your account. Activating this setting thwarts those viruses that try to replicate themselves using your e-mail program.

Another common security setting is to prevent the opening of file types that commonly carry viruses. These file types include script files, executable files, batch files, and even screen savers, which can carry malicious code.

Antivirus Software

It is important to install a good antivirus program on your system, particularly a program that checks all incoming messages for viruses. Try Norton Internet Security (www.symantec.com), McAfee Internet Security Suite (mcafee.com/us), Avast! Antivirus (www.avast.com), or AVG Internet Security (free.grisoft.com).

Guard Against Phishing Attempts

A *phishing* message is a junk e-mail message that appears to come from a legitimate organization such as a bank, a major retailer, or an Internet service provider. The message will ask you to update your information or warn you that your account is about to expire.

In most cases, the message offers a link to a Web site. That site is also configured to look legitimate, but it is just a front for the scammer. When you enter the required data — such as your credit card data, your social security number, or your online banking password — that data is sent to the scammer.

General Precautions

Never trust any e-mail message or Web site that asks you to update or confirm sensitive data such as your bank account number, credit card information, social security number, or account password. Bear in mind that no legitimate company or organization will ever contact you via e-mail to update or confirm such information online. Note, too, that some scammers also use *phone phishing* where they ask you to phone a number to update your data.

Recognize a Phishing E-mail

It is easy for a phishing scammer to craft an e-mail message that looks like it came from a legitimate organization. However, there are ways to recognize a phishing message. First, if the message is addressed to an individual, but you see [BULK] in the Subject line, then likely the message is at least spam. Second, position the mouse over any links in the message and then examine the address that appears in the status bar. If the address is clearly one that is not associated with the company, then the message is almost certainly a phishing attempt.

Turn On E-mail Phishing Filter

Windows Mail, the e-mail program that comes with Windows Vista, has a feature called the Phishing Filter that can examine received messages for signs of possible phishing activity. You should make sure that this feature is turned on. Click **Tools**, click **Junk E-mail Options**, and then click the **Phishing** tab. Select **Protect my Inbox from messages with potential Phishing links**, select **Move phishing E-mail to the Junk Mail folder**, and then click OK.

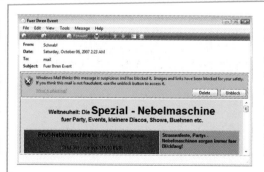

Handling Suspicious Messages

When you turn on the e-mail Phishing Filter, Windows Mail examines each incoming message for telltale phishing characteristics. If Windows Mail comes across such a message, it displays the message in red. If you open the message, you see a notice that Windows Mail believes the message to be suspicious and that it has blocked any images and links contained in the message. Unless you are sure the message is legitimate, you should click **Delete** to remove the message.

Recognize a Phishing Web Site

There are several ways to recognize if a Web page is a phishing scam. Check the address: a legitimate page will have the correct domain — such as aol.com or paypal.com — whereas a spoofed page will have only something similar. Position the mouse ⌖ over any links in the page and then look for incorrect addresses that appear in the status bar. Look for text or images not associated with the trustworthy site. Finally, if you do not see the lock icon or *https* in the address on a page that asks for financial data, the page is almost certainly a spoof.

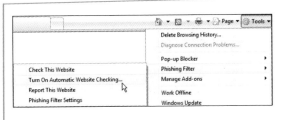

Turn On Browser Phishing Filter

To help you recognize known and suspected phishing Web sites, Internet Explorer 7 and later comes with a feature called the Phishing Filter. You should make sure that this useful feature is turned on. Click **Tools**, click **Phishing Filter**, and then examine the menu that appears. If you see the command Turn On Automatic Website Checking, click that command and then click **OK**.

Known Phishing Sites

With Internet Explorer's Phishing Filter turned on, the Web browser checks each site that you visit against a database of known phishing sites that have been reported by other users. If Internet Explorer comes across such a site, it formats the address bar area with a red background, displays Phishing Website in the address bar, and prevents you from navigating to the site.

Suspected Phishing Sites

Internet Explorer's Phishing Filter also examines each Web page that you load to see if it contains any phishing characteristics. If Internet Explorer comes across such a site, it formats the address bar area with a yellow background, and displays Suspicious Website in the address bar. Unless you are certain the site is legitimate, do not provide any information to the site.

Enhance E-mail Privacy

Enhancing e-mail privacy means taking steps to ensure that unauthorized users cannot read your messages and that senders do not know when you have read their messages.

The simplest privacy enhancements you can implement are to apply a password to your account and to deny or turn off read receipt requests.

On a more advanced level, you can obtain a digital ID to encrypt your messages. This ensures that only your recipients can read the contents of your messages.

Set Passwords

You cannot apply a password to your e-mail program, so if you share your computer with other people, they can easily open your e-mail program and read the messages that you have sent and received. The best way to prevent this is to set up separate user accounts for all the people who have access to your computer, and to configure each of those accounts with a password. Be sure to use a strong password on your account, as described in Chapter 4.

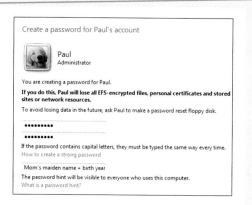

Deny Read Receipts

A *read receipt* is a short message that your e-mail program delivers to the sender when you open or preview a message from that person. The read receipt — which must be requested by the sender — informs the sender that you have viewed the message. If you consider this an invasion of privacy, click **No** when your e-mail program asks permission to send the read receipt.

Turn Off Read Receipts

If you get read receipt requests regularly, you may find that denying each request is annoying and time-consuming. Rather than deny requests individually, you can configure most e-mail programs to always deny such requests. For example, in Windows Mail and Outlook Express, click **Tools**, click **Options**, click the **Receipts** tab, click **Never send a read receipt** (◯ changes to ◉), and then click **OK**.

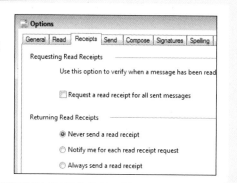

Encrypt Your E-mail

Public-Key Cryptography

An e-mail message that is in transit to the recipient can easily be intercepted and read by a person with the right tools and knowledge. To prevent this, you need to use *encryption*, which is a process that scrambles the message content to make it unreadable. A *key value* is incorporated into the encryption process, and to unscramble the message, the recipient feeds the key into the decryption process.

Public-key encryption uses two related keys: a *public key* and a *private key*. The public key is available to everyone, and the private key is secret and is stored on the user's computer. When you send a message, you use the recipient's public key to encrypt the message. The encrypted message can now only be decrypted using the recipient's private key, thus assuring privacy.

Digital ID

Before you can encrypt a message, you need to obtain a *digital ID*. This is an electronic certificate that confirms that your public key has been authenticated by a trusted certifying authority. You can then include your public key in any outgoing encrypted messages.

You can obtain a digital ID from companies such as VeriSign (digitalid.verisign.com) or GeoTrust (www.geotrust.com).

Encrypt a Message

Once you have applied your digital ID to your e-mail account, you can digitally sign an outgoing message to prove that you are the sender, and you can encrypt the message to avoid snooping and tampering. In Windows Mail and Outlook Express for example, first start a new message. To digitally sign the message, click **Tools** and then click **Digitally Sign**. A certificate icon appears to the right of the header fields. To encrypt the message, click **Tools** and then click **Encrypt**. A lock icon appears to the right of the header fields.

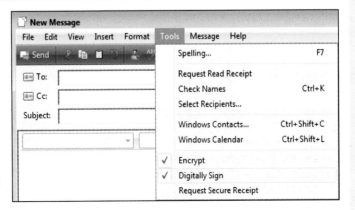

Chapter 12

Communicating via Instant Messaging and Chat

If you want to have a conversation with someone, what is the best way to go about it? The traditional method has been the telephone call, but many people resent getting phone calls because they interrupt whatever they are currently doing.

To avoid the interruption problem you might decide to use e-mail, instead. However, it is difficult to have a real conversation over e-mail because it may take minutes or even hours between responses.

To get the immediate give-and-take of a proper conversation without interrupting the other person, you need to use either instant messaging or chat. This chapter introduces you to these systems.

Introducing Instant Messaging

Instant messaging enables you to contact other people who are online, thus enabling you to have a real-time exchange of messages. Communicating in real time means that if you send a message to another person who is online, that message appears on the person's computer right away. If that person sends you a response, it appears on your computer right away.

Using an instant messaging program, you maintain a list of the people you want to chat with, and those people must also use the same program. The program monitors each person's online status, and you can only start a chat with someone who is currently available.

Instant Messaging Programs

To send and receive instant messages, you must use an instant messaging program. Windows Vista offers a link to the Windows Live Messenger program, Windows XP comes with Windows Messenger, and Mac OS X comes with iChat. Other programs include AOL Instant Messenger (www.aim.com), Yahoo! Messenger (messenger.yahoo.com), and ICQ (www.icq.com).

System Compatibility

The biggest problem with instant messaging systems is that they are generally not compatible with each other. With very few exceptions — for example, Windows Live Messenger works with Yahoo! Messenger and iChat works with AOL Instant Messenger — you cannot send instant messages between different systems. One solution is to download an all-in-one program such as Easy Message (www.easymessage.net) or Trillian (www.ceruleanstudios.com) that works with all instant messaging systems.

Contact List

You send instant messages to, and receive instant messages from, the people in your *contact list*, which is also called a *buddy list*. Your instant messaging program enables you to maintain your contact list by adding and deleting people, and it tells you the current online status of each person on the list.

Online Notification

Instant messages are "instant" because both parties are online at the same time, and so the program delivers the messages in real time. Therefore, all instant messaging programs notify you when a person who is in your contacts list comes online. In most cases, the icon associated with the buddy changes to reflect the new status. In Windows Live Messenger, for example, the contact icon turns green.

Online Status

If you do not want to receive any messages for a while, you can change your status accordingly. For example, Windows Live Messenger gives you several status settings, including Available, Busy, Away, and Appear Offline. On the Mac, the iChat program shown here has even more status settings.

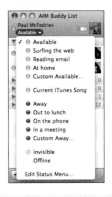

Block a Sender

If you no longer want to receive messages from a particular sender, all instant message programs enable you to block that sender. This means that the program will no longer allow messages from that person to go through. Blocking a sender is useful when that person becomes annoying, abusive, or offensive.

Discover Instant Messaging Systems

To exchange instant messages with another person, you must have access to an instant messaging (IM) system, and that system must be compatible with the system that the other person is using.

Most instant messaging systems are software programs that you install on your computer. These systems include Windows Live Messenger for Windows and iChat for the Mac. Systems that have both Windows and Mac versions include AOL Instant Messenger, Yahoo! Messenger, and ICQ.

There are also Web-based instant messaging systems that enable you to access your account and exchange messages from any computer.

Windows Live Messenger

Windows Live Messenger is Microsoft's flagship IM system and it offers a wide variety of features. Besides sending instant messages, you can also use Windows Live Messenger to place phone calls to a computer or phone, conduct video chats, exchange files, play games, and more. You can download Windows Live Messenger from get.live.com/messenger.

iChat

iChat is the IM system that comes with every version of Mac OS X. With iChat, you can exchange instant messages with iChat, AOL Instant Messenger, Google Talk, and Jabber users over the Internet, and with other iChat users over your network. You can also use iChat to conduct audio chats and video chats, send e-mail messages, exchange files, share your desktop, and more.

Windows Messenger

Windows Messenger is the IM system that comes with Windows XP. With Windows Messenger you can exchange instant messages, conduct a video conversation, send someone a file or photo, send an e-mail message, share an application with another user, and collaborate by writing messages on a whiteboard.

AOL Instant Messenger

AOL Instant Messenger (AIM) is the America Online instant messaging system. You can use it to exchange messages with other AIM users as well as with iChat users who have MobileMe accounts. AIM also enables you to have voice and video chats, exchange files and pictures, send e-mail messages, and more. You can download AIM from www.aim.com.

Yahoo! Messenger

Yahoo! Messenger is the Yahoo! instant messaging system. You can use it to exchange messages with other Yahoo! users as well as with Windows Live Messenger users. Yahoo! Messenger also enables you to have voice and video chats, swap files and photos, send e-mail messages, and more. To download Yahoo! Messenger, go to messenger.yahoo.com.

ICQ

ICQ (pronounced "I seek you") is one of the oldest instant messaging systems, and it has millions of users. You can use it to exchange messages with other ICQ users as well as AIM users. ICQ also enables you to have voice and video chats, exchange files and pictures, send e-mail messages, and more. You can download ICQ from www.icq.com.

Web Instant Messaging

Although most people send instant messages using a software program on their computer, you can also exchange instant messages via the Web. The most popular sites are Google Talk (www.google.com/talk) and MSN Web Messenger (webmessenger.msn.com). There are also Web-based services that support multiple instant messaging services, including meebo (www.meebo.com), Communication Tube (www.communicationtube.com), and eBuddy (www.ebuddy.com).

Instant Messaging with Windows

To exchange instant messages in Windows, you need to download, install, and configure an instant messaging system such as Windows Live Messenger.

Although almost all IM systems come with versions for Windows Vista and Windows XP, most Windows users use Microsoft's Windows Live Messenger system. You can download this system from get.live.com/messenger, but there is also a Start menu link in Windows Vista that takes you to the download page (click Start, then All Programs, then Windows Live Messenger Download). You will also need a Windows Live ID, which you can sign up for at home.live.com.

Instant Messaging with Windows

SIGN IN TO WINDOWS LIVE MESSENGER

① Click the **Windows Live Messenger** icon.

② Click **Sign in**.

③ Use the **E-mail address** text box to type your Windows Live ID address.

⬤ Click here to save your address (☐ changes to ☑).

④ Use the **Password** text box to type your Windows Live ID password.

⬤ Click here to save your password (☐ changes to ☑).

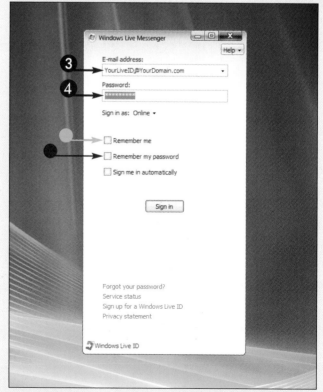

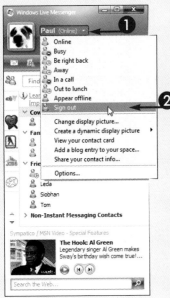

5 Click **Sign in**.

Windows Live Messenger signs in to your account.

● Click here to have Windows Live Messenger sign in to your account automatically (☐ changes to ☑).

SIGN OUT OF WINDOWS LIVE MESSENGER

1 Click your current status.

2 Click **Sign out**.

Windows Live Messenger signs you out of your account.

How do I change my display name and my picture?
Sign in to your Windows Live Messenger account, click your current status, and then click **Options**. In the Options dialog box, click the **Personal** tab, then edit the **Type your name as you want others to see it** text box. Click the **Change Picture** button and then click a picture. To use one of your own images, click **Browse**, click the picture, and then click **Open**. Click **OK** to return to the Options dialog box, and then click **OK**.

How do I prevent Windows Live Messenger from displaying the Windows Live Today window after I sign in?
Sign in to your Windows Live Messenger account, click your current status, and then click **Options**. In the Options dialog box, click the **General** tab. Click the **Show Windows Live Today after I sign in to Messenger** check box (☑ changes to ☐), and then click **OK**.

Instant Messaging with the Mac

Although there are many instant messaging systems for the Mac, most Mac users exchange instant messages using the iChat application that comes with each Mac. To use iChat, you need to configure it with your account data.

iChat supports four different IM account types: Apple's MobileMe service; AOL Instant Messenger; Google Talk; and Jabber. In each case, you need to know your account's user name and password.

Note, too, that you can also use iChat to exchange messages with other iChat users on your network. You do not need to configure an account for network-based chats.

Instant Messaging with the Mac

1 Click the **iChat** icon (🖻) in the Dock.

Your Mac launches the iChat application.

2 Click **iChat**.

3 Click **Preferences**.

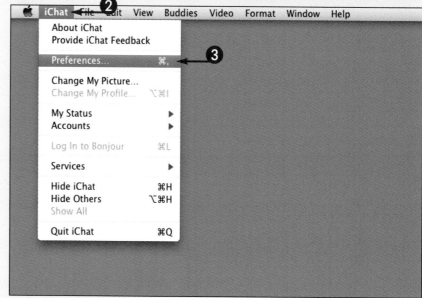

204

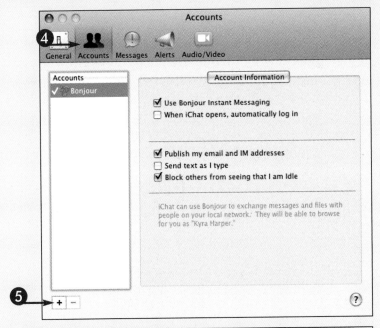

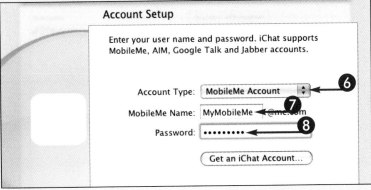

The iChat preferences appear.

4 Click **Accounts**.

5 Click **Add Account** (⊞).

6 Click ⊞ and then click the IM account type you have.

7 Type your IM account user name.

8 Type your IM account password.

9 Click **Done** at the bottom of the window (not shown).

iChat adds the account.

Note: *For a MobileMe account, when iChat asks if you want to use encryption, click **Continue**.*

Simplify It

Can I get an iChat ID without having to pay for a MobileMe account?
Yes. Follow steps **1** to **5**, and then click the **Get an iChat Account** button. Your Mac launches Safari and takes you to a page called Create your iChat ID. Type the **iChat ID** you want to use, fill in your password, e-mail address, name, and other requested data, and then click **Continue**.

How do I change my display name and my picture?
Click the **Address Book** icon (📖) in the Dock, and then choose **Card** and then **Go to My Card**. Click **Edit** to open your card for editing. Type your first name, press Tab, and then type your last name. To change your picture, double-click the existing picture, click **Choose**, click the picture you want to use, and then click **Open**. Click **Set** to return to the card, and then click **Edit** to save your changes.

Add a Buddy

You send instant messages to, and receive instant messages from, the people in your *buddy list*, which is also called a *contact list*. Before you can send an instant message to a person, you must add the person to your instant messaging program's buddy list.

With Windows Live Messenger, you can add buddies that have either a Windows Live ID or a Yahoo! Messenger ID. With iChat, if you are using a MobileMe or AIM account, you can add MobileMe or AIM buddies; if you are using a Google Talk or Jabber account, you can add Google Talk or Jabber buddies.

Add a Buddy

ADD A BUDDY IN WINDOWS LIVE MESSENGER

① Click **Add a contact** (🖳).

The Add a Contact dialog box appears.

② Use the **Instant Messaging Address** text box to type your buddy's IM address.

③ Use the **Nickname** text box to type a display name for your buddy.

④ In the **Group** list, click ⊡ and then click a group.

⑤ Click **Add contact**.

Windows Live Messenger adds the person to your buddy list.

Note: *The other person must click* ***Allow*** *(◎ changes to ◉) and then click* ***OK*** *to confirm.*

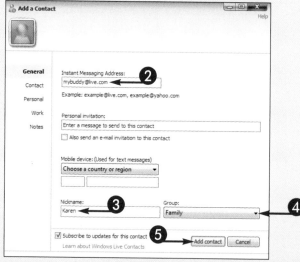

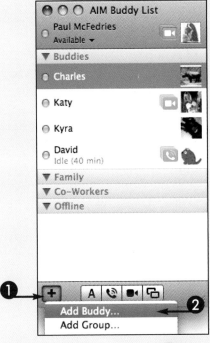

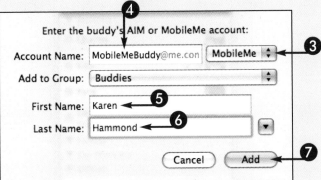

ADD A BUDDY IN ICHAT

1 Click **Add** (⊞).

2 Click **Add Buddy**.

> *Note: You can also run the Add Buddy command by pressing* `Shift` + `⌘` + `A`.

3 In the pop-up menu beside the Account Name text box, click ⬦ and then click your buddy's account type.

4 Use the **Account Name** text box to specify your buddy's account name.

5 Use the **First Name** text box to type your buddy's first name.

6 Use the **Last Name** text box to type your buddy's last name.

7 Click **Add**.

> iChat adds the person to your buddy list.

Simplify It

How do I make changes to a buddy's information?
In Windows Live Messenger, if you want to change only the buddy's nickname, click the buddy, press `F2`, type the new name, and then press `Enter`. To edit other data, right-click the buddy, click **Edit contact**, make your changes, and then click **Save**. In iChat, right-click (or `Control` + click) the buddy, click **Show Info**, click **Address Card**, and then edit the data.

Is there a way to change the picture that iChat uses for my buddy?
Yes. By default, iChat uses whatever picture your buddy has configured for himself or herself. To display a different picture, right-click (or `Control` + click) the buddy, click **Show Info**, click **Address Card**, click **Always use this picture** (☐ changes to ☑), and then click and drag the picture you want to use and drop it on the Picture box.

Carry On a Text Chat

In any instant messaging system, an IM conversation is most often the exchange of text messages between two or more people who are online and available to chat.

An instant messaging conversation begins by one person inviting another person to exchange messages. In a program such as Windows Live Messenger or iChat, this process begins by sending an initial instant message to a person who is online. When the other person receives the initial message, he or she can either accept or reject the invitation. If the person accepts the invitation, he or she then sends a response, and the conversation continues.

Carry On a Text Chat

SEND A CHAT INVITATION

❶ In your buddy list, make sure the person's status icon is green, which means that the person is available to chat.

❷ Double-click the person you want to chat with.

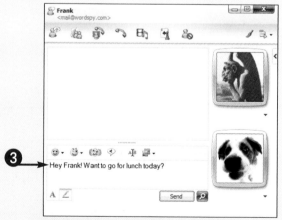

A chat window appears.

❸ Type your invitation or opening message.

❹ Press `Enter` or `Return`.

The invitation appears on the other person's computer.

ACCEPT A CHAT INVITATION

❶ Click the invitation.

Note: *If the person who sent the message is not on your buddy list, iChat does not display the message. To see the message, you must click* **Display**.

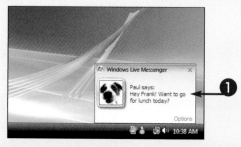

2 Type a response.

3 Press Enter or Return.

Note: To decline the invitation, instead, close the chat window or, in iChat, click **Decline**.

● The response appears in the chat window.

4 Repeat steps **3** and **4** from the previous page to continue chatting.

The chat text is too small. How do I make it bigger?
If you are having trouble reading the chat text, you can enlarge the font size. In Windows Live Messenger, press Alt to display the menu bar, click **Tools**, click **Text Size**, and then click the size you prefer, such as **Larger** or **Largest**. In iChat, click **Format** and then click **Show Fonts** to display the Fonts window. Use the **Size** list to click the font size you prefer.

Is there a way to automatically decline a person who is bothering me?
Yes, there is. If you no longer want to receive messages from a sender who is annoying, abusive, or offensive, your IM program enables you to block that sender. This means that the program will no longer allow messages from that person to go through. In Windows Live Messenger, right-click the person and then click **Block contact**. In iChat, when a chat alert message comes through from that person, click the message and then click **Block**. When iChat asks you to confirm, click **Block** again.

Perform an Audio Chat

Most instant messaging systems come with an *audio chat* feature that enables you to speak to another person over the Internet.

To conduct an audio chat, you and the buddy with whom you want to converse both require a microphone attached to your computers, a sound card inside your computers, and speakers connected to the sound card. If both of you have all of these components, you can converse with each other just as though you were talking over the phone.

Note that almost all Macs come with built-in sound cards, and many also have built-in microphones.

Perform an Audio Chat

SEND AN AUDIO CHAT INVITATION

1 In your buddy list, make sure the person's status icon is green, which means that the person is available to chat.

2 Right-click the person you want to chat with.

3 Click **Call**.

4 Click **Call computer**.

> **Note:** *In iChat, click **Invite to Audio Chat**.*

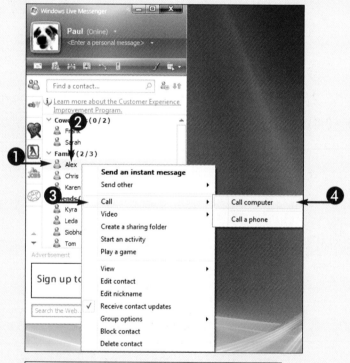

> **Note:** *In Windows Live Messenger, if you see the Audio and Video Setup wizard, click **Next** in each dialog box.*

An audio chat window appears and your IM program waits for a response to the invitation.

The invitation appears on the other person's computer.

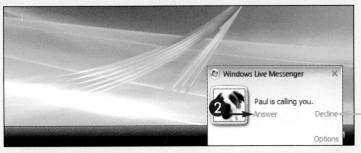

ACCEPT AN AUDIO CHAT INVITATION

1 Click the invitation.

2 Click **Answer**.

*Note: In iChat, click **Accept**, instead. If you prefer to text chat, click **Text Reply** to begin a separate text chat.*

● If you cannot chat right now, click **Decline**.

Your IM program sets up the audio connection.

3 Use your microphone to converse with the other person.

● You can click and drag the slider to control the chat volume.

4 In Windows Live Messenger, when you have completed the chat, click **Hang up**.

I added a headset to my computer. How can I hear my audio chats through the headset instead of the speakers?

You need to configure your IM system to use the headset as the output device. In Windows Live Messenger, press Alt to display the menu bar, click **Tools**, and then click **Audio and video setup**. Click **Next**, click ⊡ in the Speaker Setup dialog box, click your headset, and then complete the wizard. In iChat, click **iChat**, click **Preferences**, click the **Audio/Video** tab, click the **Sound Output** ⊡, and then click your headset.

Is there a way to turn off the ringing sound that plays when an audio chat invitation comes in?

Yes, you can configure your IM system to not play the sound. In Windows Live Messenger, press Alt to display the menu bar, click **Tools**, and then click **Options**. Click **Sounds**, click **Incoming voice or video call**, click the **Don't play sound** option (○ changes to ◉), and then click **OK**. In iChat, click **iChat**, click **Preferences**, click the **Alerts** tab, and then click the **Play sound** check box (☑ changes to ☐).

Communicate with a Video Chat

Many instant messaging systems offer a *video chat* feature that enables you to see each other's Web camera image and hear each other's voice over the Internet.

To communicate using a video chat, you and the buddy with whom you want to converse both require special equipment connected to your computer. You both need a Web camera for the video feed, and a microphone, sound card, and speakers for the audio portion. If you both have all of these components, you can see and talk to each other from any location.

Note that many Macs come with built-in iSight cameras.

Communicate with a Video Chat

SEND A VIDEO CHAT INVITATION

1 In your buddy list, make sure the person's status icon is green, which means that the person is available to chat.

2 Right-click the person you want to chat with.

3 Click **Video**.

4 Click **Start a Video Call**.

Note: In iChat, click **Invite to Video Chat**.

Note: In Windows Live Messenger, if you see the Audio and Video Setup wizard, click **Next** in each dialog box.

A video chat window appears and your IM program waits for a response to the invitation.

The invitation appears on the other person's computer.

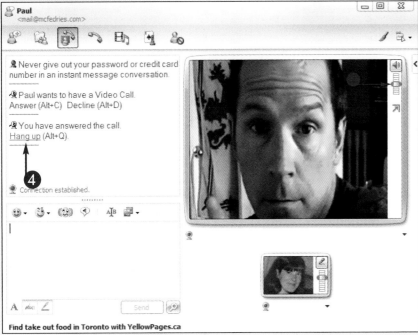

Find take out food in Toronto with YellowPages.ca

ACCEPT A VIDEO CHAT INVITATION

① Click the invitation.

② Click **Answer**.

*Note: In iChat, click **Accept**, instead. If you prefer to text chat, click **Text Reply** to begin a separate text chat.*

● If you cannot chat right now, click **Decline**.

Your IM program sets up the video connection.

③ Use your microphone to converse with the other person.

● You can click and drag the slider to control the chat volume.

④ In Windows Live Messenger, when you have completed the chat, click **Hang up**.

I do not have a Web camera, but my buddy does. Is it possible to see her video?
Yes, you can set up a one-way video chat where you can see your buddy's video feed. Follow the steps in this section to send an invitation to your buddy. When that person accepts your invitation, you will see his or her video feed. You can converse with your buddy either by using the microphone for an audio chat, or by typing messages for a text chat.

Is it possible to see a larger version of my buddy's video feed?
Yes, you can configure your IM system to play the video using a larger window or the entire screen. In Windows Live Messenger, click the ⊡ below the buddy's video feed, click **Size**, and then click **Full Screen**.

In iChat, you can resize the video window to make it larger. For the full-screen view, click **Video** and then click **Full Screen**. (You can also press Control + ⌘ + F.)

Converse in an Internet Chat Room

If you do not have an instant messaging program installed on your computer, you can still chat with other people by using an Internet chat room.

The Internet offers thousands of chat rooms that cover hundreds of different topics. Many chat rooms are dedicated to singles looking for relationships, but there are also dedicated chat rooms for teens, hobbyists, businesspeople, or anyone looking for an informal social connection.

To get the most out of Internet chat rooms, you need to know how the rooms work, how to chat, and the basics of chat etiquette and safety.

Chat Room Basics

Almost all Internet chat rooms are free, and some do not require you to sign up or create an account. In most cases, you locate the chat room you want to use, enter a nickname or user name, and then start chatting. On most sites you need to create an account that lets you use a permanent nickname, create a profile, post a photo, and receive other privileges.

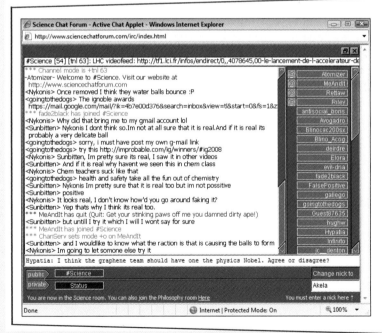

Chat Basics

Once you have entered the chat room of your choice, you usually see a list of the other people who are currently chatting, and the bulk of the window shows the messages as they are posted. There will also be a text box where you can type your messages. In most cases, you type your text and then press Enter or Return to send the message. If your message is aimed at a particular person, precede the message with that person's name.

Chat Etiquette

To help make Internet chat a pleasant experience for you and for the people you converse with, you need to know about chat etiquette, sometimes shortened to *chatiquette*. For example, you should always introduce yourself to a new chat group. For your messages, keep them short, stay on topic (if there is one), avoid profanity and advertising, and do not type entirely in UPPERCASE LETTERS because they make it look like you are shouting. Also, do not ask a stranger for personal information such as a person's age or location. Finally, always be courteous and respectful to other chatters.

Chat Safety

Internet chat rooms are generally safe places, and you should not run into any problems using them. However, there are a few precautions you should take. For example, do not use your real name, never give out personal information such as your phone number or address, and never divulge confidential information such as your credit card number or social security number.

Adults who desire to meet young children often frequent Internet chat rooms and attempt to get young participants to reveal personal details about themselves, particularly where they live or where they go to school. This means you should educate your children about these potential dangers and lay down ground rules for using chat (such as not giving out personal data to strangers without permission).

Java Chat Rooms

You interact with many of the Internet's chat rooms by using an applet written in the Java programming language. Browsers such as Internet Explorer and Firefox do not come with built-in Java support, so you must install it. Go to java.com/en/download, click **Free Java Download**, and then follow the instructions for installing Java.

Chapter 13

Creating and Reading Blogs

Weblogs — better known as just *blogs* — are a true Internet phenomenon. There are well over 100 million blogs on the Web, up from about 4 million in 2004.

That so many people have their own blog is a testament to the need many people feel to publish their ideas, opinions, and stories. It is very difficult to break into traditional print publishing, but with the blogging tools now available, it is very easy to get into online publishing.

If you are more into reading what others have published, with millions of blogs available, there are bound to be many that have content that interests you.

Understanding Blogs

Blogging is an exciting and dynamic online medium, and if you are interested in blogging then you are probably anxious to get going. However, before you get started with blogging, it is a good idea to take a second and understand a few key concepts. Besides understanding just what a blog is, you also need to know about posts and posting, and you need to understand the basics behind bloggers, blogging, and blog hosting services.

This section also introduces you to a few other key blog concepts, including comments, archives, permalinks, and trackbacks.

What Is a Blog?

A blog is a Web site that consists of a frequently updated collection of entries, displayed in reverse chronological order (that is, with the most recent entries at the top). Most blogs focus on a particular topic or subject area, although on the majority of blogs the "subject" is the person writing the blog. The first "Web logs" appeared in the mid 1990s and consisted of lists — or *logs* — of where a person had been on the Web. As a result, almost all blogs frequently link to and comment on other sites and other blogs.

Posts and Posting

The individual entries that appear on a blog are called *posts*, and the act of publishing a blog entry is called *posting*. Most posts consist of a title, the text of the entry, the date and time it was posted, the name of the person who posted it, and one or more keywords — usually called *tags* — that serve to categorize the post. Most blogs are updated a few times per week, but many blogs are updated with several posts per day.

Bloggers

Most blogs are maintained by a single person, and that person is referred to as a *blogger*. Some blogs allow other people to post occasional entries, and those people are known as *guest bloggers*. There are also many blogs that have multiple authors. One of the most popular blogs on the Internet is Boing Boing (www.boingboing.net), which has five bloggers.

Blogging

Although modern blog hosting services make it easy to set up, configure, and post to a blog, maintaining a consistent blogging schedule is hard. Of the more than 100 million existing blogs, only about five percent have been updated in the previous four months, which underlines the fact that most blogs are abandoned after a while. If you want to start a blog, make sure you pick a topic that interests you and that will enable you to post fresh content regularly without taking up too much of your time.

Blog Hosting Services

Although you can build a blog from scratch using the standard HTML tags used for almost all Web pages, it is faster and easier to use a blog hosting service. This is a Web site that enables you to quickly create and configure a full-featured blog and then easily post to that blog. Among the blog hosting services that you learn about in this chapter are Blogger (www.blogger.com), TypePad (www.typepad.com), and WordPress (www. wordpress.com).

Comments

Most blogs support *comments*, which are responses that people other than the blogger write in reaction to a blog post (although the blogger can also post a comment in response to a comment). In most cases, the comments appear below the original post, although in some cases they appear on a separate page.

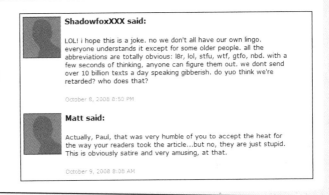

More Blogging Terms

A blog *archive* is a database of all the blog's posts, particularly previous posts that no longer appear on the blog's main page, which shows only the most recent posts. A *permalink* is a link to a post in a blog's archive. A *trackback* is a link to a blog post from some other site. A *blogroll* is a list of links to the blogs that a blogger reads regularly or recommends. The *blogosphere* is the collection of all bloggers, blog sites, blog readers, and blog text.

Blog with Blogger

More than any other tool, the blog hosting service Blogger (www.blogger.com) spurred the rapid rise of the blogging phenomenon. Blogger was launched in 1999, and it enabled people who did not want to learn the syntax of HTML to focus on researching and writing instead of the nuts and bolts of blogging.

Blogger's ease of use enabled anyone to get on the blog bandwagon, and many thousands of people did just that.

In 2003, Blogger was acquired by Google, which has steadily added new features and kept Blogger at the forefront of blog hosting.

BLOGGER FEATURES

Blogger is a free and full-featured blog hosting service that offers just about everything that a new blogger could ask for. You get extensive formatting and layout options; complete control over comments; syndication of your blog to a feed; the ability to post via e-mail, mobile phone, and the Google toolbar; and the option to use multiple blog authors.

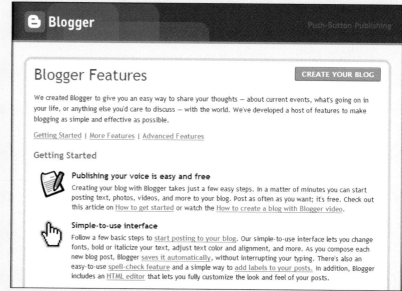

CREATE A BLOG

① Go to www.blogger.com.

② Click **Create Your Blog Now**.

● If you already have a Google account, type your account's e-mail address and password, and then click **Sign in**. You then type just the display name you want to use and click **Continue**.

Note: *If you do not have a Google account, you need to create one to use Blogger, as described next.*

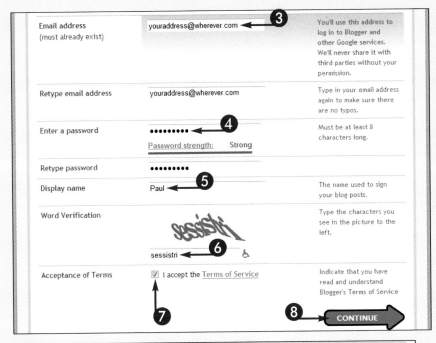

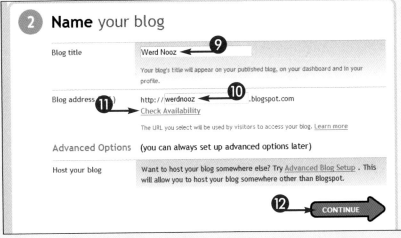

❸ Type your e-mail address in the two text boxes.

❹ Type the password you want to use in the two boxes.

❺ Type the display name you want to use.

❻ Type the characters you see.

❼ Click the acceptance of terms check box (☐ changes to ☑).

❽ Click **Continue**.

The next step is to set up your blog.

❾ Use the **Blog title** text box to provide a name for your blog, which will appear at the top of each page.

❿ Use the **Blog address (URL)** text box to type the address you want to use.

This address uses the form http://*youraddress*/blogspot.com, where *youraddress* is the address you type.

⓫ Click **Check Availability** to ensure the address is available.

⓬ Click **Continue**.

Simplify It

Can I customize my blog after it is created?
Yes, your blog offers a number of settings that you can customize, including the blog title, BlogSpot address, comment options, and the site feed. In any Blogger page, click **Settings** and then click a category. You can also customize the look of your blog by changing the page layout, selecting new fonts and colors, or choosing a different template. In any Blogger page, click **Layout** and then click a category. If you are viewing your blog, click **Customize** and then click either **Settings** or **Layout**.

Blog with Blogger
(continued)

When you sign in to your Blogger account, your home page includes the Dashboard, which lists your blogs and offers quick links to some common blogging features.

For example, Blogger offers twelve predesigned templates that govern the look and layout of your blog. You can change the design later on, but for now you must select the template you want to start with.

Once your blog is created, you can start posting messages to it. Blogger helps here by offering you several ways to post. The most straightforward is to log in to Blogger and post from your account. However, you can also post using the Google toolbar, via e-mail, and via mobile phone.

Blog with Blogger (continued)

The Choose a template page appears.

⑬ Click the design you prefer (◎ changes to ◉).

● If you are not sure, click the **preview template** link under a design to see a sample in a separate window.

⑭ Click **Continue**.

Blogger creates your blog

⑮ Click **Start Blogging**.

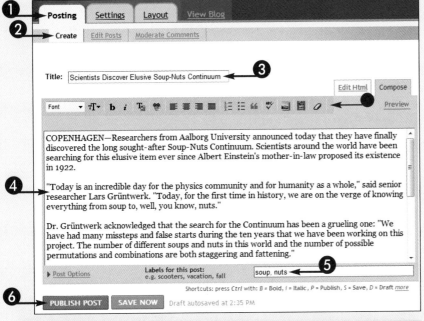

POST TO YOUR BLOG

1 Click **Posting**.

2 Click **Create**.

*Note: In the Blogger Dashboard, click **New Post**, instead.*

3 Use the **Title** text box to type a post title.

4 Use the large text box to type the body of the post.

● You can use the icons to format the text.

5 Use the **Labels for this post** text box to type one or more tags, separated by commas.

6 When you are done, click **Publish Post**.

VIEW YOUR BLOG

Blogger gives you a couple of ways to view your blog.

1 In any of your Blogger pages, click the **View Blog** link.

From outside of Blogger, use your Web browser to navigate to your BlogSpot address: http://*youraddress*.blogspot.com, where *youraddress* is the address you specified when you created the blog.

Simplify It

Are there other ways that I can post to my blog?
Yes, Blogger offers three other methods for posting to your blog. If you have the Google toolbar installed (see www.google.com/toolbar), navigate to a page, click **Sent to**, and then click **Blogger**. To configure e-mail posting, log in to Blogger, click **Settings**, click **Email**, type an address in the **Mail-to-Blogger Address** text box, and then click **Save Settings**. To post via mobile phone, send a message to go@blogger.com and then note the claim code that is sent back. Then go to go.blogger.com and enter the claim code.

Set Up a TypePad Blog

TypePad (www.typepad.com) is one of the Web's most popular blog hosting services, with more than 40 million users. This popularity is not surprising because TypePad offers an inexpensive hosting service loaded with useful and innovative features.

With TypePad, you can create a new blog in just a few minutes, and you can configure it with a professional-looking design with just a few mouse clicks.

For as little as $4.95 per month, TypePad offers easy posting (including the ability to post via e-mail or mobile phone), lots of storage space, and impressive safety features. A free 14-day trial enables you to test-drive TypePad before committing.

Set Up a TypePad Blog

TYPEPAD FEATURES

All TypePad subscriptions offer a wide range of features, including a simple interface for publishing posts; blog design customization; posting via e-mail or a mobile phone; complete control over comments; syndication of your blog to a feed or podcast; comprehensive site statistics; and small applications called widgets to add features to your blog such as games, videos, and chat. The Pro, Premium, and Business Class subscriptions also offer the option to use multiple blog authors.

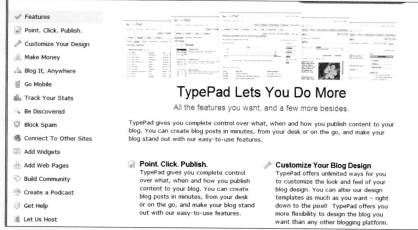

CREATE A TYPEPAD BLOG

① Go to www.typepad.com.

② Click **Free Trial: Sign Up Now**.

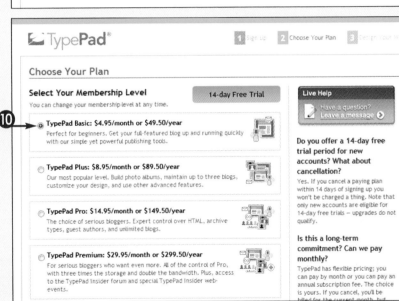

③ Type your e-mail address.

④ Type the password you want to use.

⑤ Type your first name.

⑥ Type your last name.

⑦ Specify your birth date.

⑧ Use the **Create Your Blog Address** text box to type the address you want to use.

This address uses the form http://*youraddress*.typepad.com, where *youraddress* is the address you type.

⑨ Click **Create Your Account** (not shown).

⑩ Click the membership level you want to use if you decide to stick with TypePad after your 14-day free trial expires (◎ changes to ◉).

⑪ Fill in your credit card information and billing address (not shown).

⑫ Click **Next** (not shown).

Simplify It

Do I have to pay for a TypePad account?
Yes. Although TypePad offers a 14-day free trial, when that time is up you must switch to a paid subscription. TypePad offers five subscription levels: Basic, Plus, Pro, Premium, and Business Class. The Basic subscription at just $4.95 per month (or $49.50 per year) offers more than enough features for most beginning bloggers.

continued

Set Up a TypePad Blog *(continued)*

TypePad offers dozens of predesigned templates that govern the fonts, colors, and backgrounds used on your blog. You can change the design later on, but for now you must select the template you want to start with.

Once you have created your TypePad blog, you can start posting messages right away. TypePad makes this easier by offering you several ways to post. The most straightforward is to log in to TypePad and post from your account. However, you can also post via e-mail and via mobile phone.

Set Up a TypePad Blog *(continued)*

⑬ Type your blog title.

⑭ Click an option in the **Choose a Layout** area (◎ changes to ⦿).

⑮ Click the **Choose a Theme** ▾ and then click a theme.

⑯ Click the template (◎ changes to ⦿).

⑰ Click **Next** (not shown).

⑱ Click **Continue** (not shown).

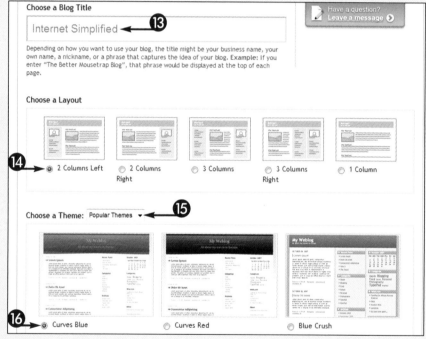

⑲ Click **Get Started**.

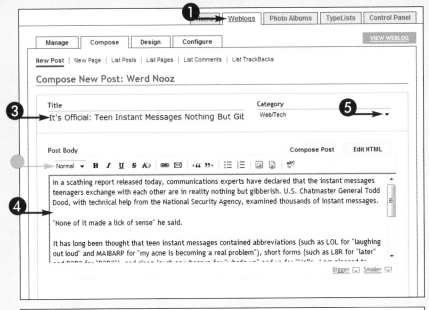

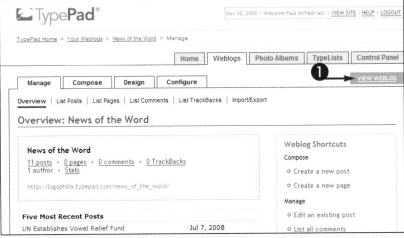

POST TO YOUR BLOG

① Click **Weblogs**.

② Click **Begin a new post** (not shown).

③ Use the **Title** text box to type a title for the post.

④ Use the large text box to type the body of the post.

● You can use the icons to format the text in various ways.

⑤ Use the **Category** ☑ to choose or create a post category.

⑥ Click **Save** (not shown).

VIEW YOUR BLOG

TypePad gives you a couple of ways to view your blog.

① In any of your TypePad pages, click the **View Weblog** link.

From outside of TypePad, use your Web browser to navigate to your TypePad address: http://*youraddress*.typepad. com, where *youraddress* is the address you specified when you created the blog.

Simplify It

Can I customize my TypePad blog after I create it?
TypePad offers a number of settings that you can customize, including the theme, layout, and title. Click the **Weblogs** tab, click your blog title, and then click **Design**. From here you can modify the theme, layout, and content. Click **Republish Weblog** when you are done. You can also click **Configure** to modify things like the blog name and description.

To set up mobile blogging via e-mail or mobile phone, click **Control Panel**, click **Profile**, and then click **Mobile Settings**.

Create a WordPress Blog

WordPress (www.wordpress.com) is a popular blog hosting service, with more than 4 million blogs. WordPress offers a free version that still gives you many useful and innovative features and lots of storage space. There are also various premium features such as extra storage, custom domain names, and ad-free pages that you can pay for.

With WordPress, you can create a new blog quickly, post very easily, and customize your blog with a professional-looking design in just a few mouse clicks.

Create a WordPress Blog

CREATE A WORDPRESS BLOG

1 Go to wordpress.com.

2 Click **Sign Up Now**.

3 Type the user name you want to use.

4 Type the password you want to use.

5 Type your e-mail address.

6 Click the **Gimme a blog!** option (◎ changes to ◉).

7 Click **Next**.

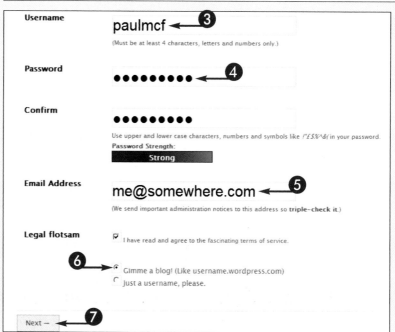

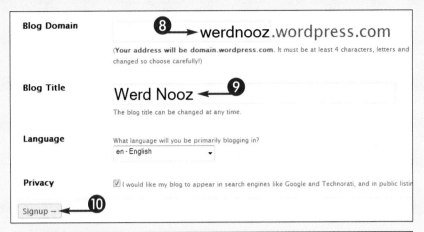

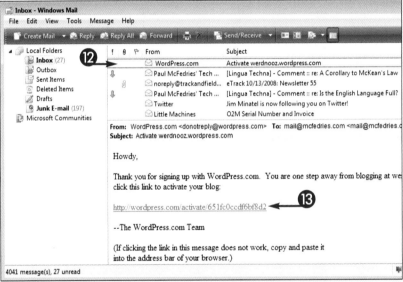

8 Use the **Blog Domain** text box to type the address you want to use.

This address uses the form http://*youraddress*.wordpress. com, where *youraddress* is the address you type.

9 Use the **Blog Title** text box to type the title you want to use for your blog.

10 Click **Signup**.

11 Open your e-mail program.

12 Click the message from WordPress.com.

13 Click the link.

WordPress activates your account.

How do I customize my WordPress profile?
Your WordPress profile controls data such as your name, password, and picture. Go to wordpress.com, log in to your WordPress account, and then click your blog name. In the top left corner of the WordPress screen, click **My Account** and then click **Edit Profile**. Use text boxes such as **First name**, **Last name**, and **Biographical Info** to update your profile data. To upload a profile picture, click **Browse** in the My Picture section, select an image using the Choose File dialog box, click **Open**, and then click **Upload Image**.

continued

Create a WordPress Blog *(continued)*

WordPress is a free and full-featured blog hosting service that offers everything that any new or experienced blogger could want. You get extensive formatting and layout options; complete control over comments; syndication of your blog to a feed; comprehensive site statistics; the option to use multiple blog authors; and small applications called widgets

to add features to your blog such as games, photos, and chat.

WordPress offers dozens of predesigned themes that govern the layout, fonts, colors, and backgrounds used on your blog. WordPress applies the default theme when you create your blog, but you can change the theme at any time.

Create a WordPress Blog (continued)

CHOOSE A BLOG THEME

1 Click **Design**.

2 Click a theme.

WordPress displays a preview of the theme in a new window.

3 If you want to use that theme, click the **Activate *"Theme"*** link (where *Theme* is the name of the theme).

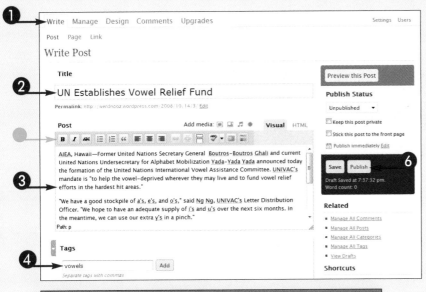

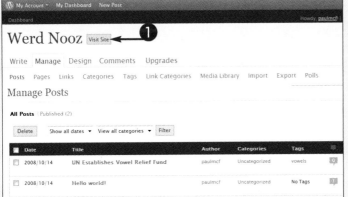

POST TO YOUR BLOG

❶ Click **Write**.

❷ Use the **Title** text box to type a title for the post.

❸ Use the large text box to type the body of the post.

⬤ You can use the icons to format the text in various ways.

❹ Use the **Tags** text box to specify one or more tags.

❺ Use the **Category** section (not shown) to choose or create a post category.

❻ Click **Publish**.

VIEW YOUR BLOG

WordPress gives you two ways to view your blog.

❶ In any of your WordPress pages, click the **Visit Site** link.

From outside of WordPress, use your Web browser to navigate to your WordPress address: http://*youraddress*.wordpress. com, where *youraddress* is the address you specified when you created the blog.

Simplify It

Can I customize my WordPress blog after I create it?
WordPress offers a number of settings that you can customize, including the blog title and subtitle (which WordPress calls the *tagline*), post settings, privacy settings, and much more. Click **Settings** and then click the various tabs to view the different settings: **General**, **Writing**, **Reading**, and so on. In each tab, when you are done with your modifications, click **Save Changes**.

Microblog with Twitter

Twitter (www.twitter.com) is a service that enables you to create your own page for *microblogging*, a form of blogging where each post is a very short message. In Twitter's case, all messages have a limit of 140 characters.

Each Twitter post is ostensibly an answer to the same basic question: "What are you doing?"

This means that many people use Twitter as a kind of short-form diary to post constant updates — called *tweets* — about activities, thoughts, and feelings. However, many people also use Twitter to point out other interesting Web sites and to send direct messages to other Twitter users.

Microblog with Twitter

CREATE A TWITTER ACCOUNT

To use Twitter, you must sign up for a free account.

1 Go to www.twitter.com.

2 Click the **Get Started—Join!** link.

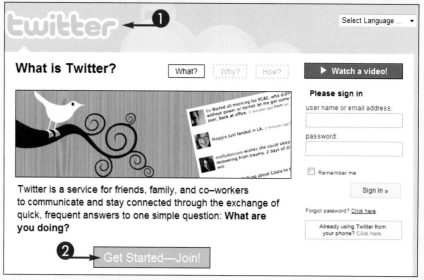

The Create a Free Twitter Account page appears.

3 Use the **Username** text box to type the user name you want to use.

Twitter checks the availability of the name, and you will need to try again if the name is already taken.

4 Type the password you want to use.

5 Type your e-mail address.

6 Type the displayed words.

7 Click **I accept. Create my account.**

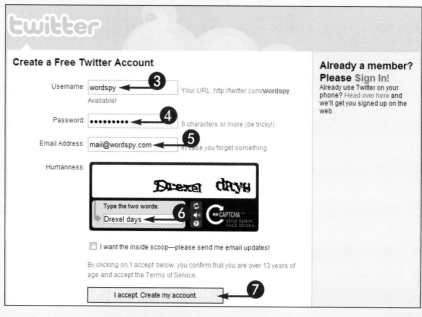

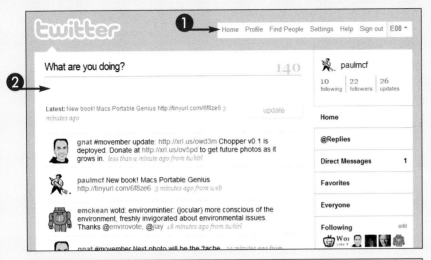

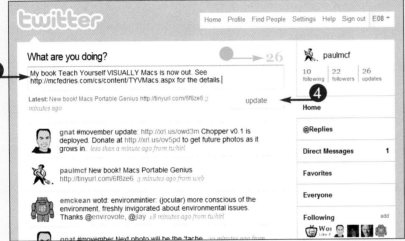

SEND A TWEET

With your account set up, you can now send tweets (which Twitter also calls *updates*).

① Click **Home**.

② Click inside the **What are you doing?** text box.

③ Type a message that is a maximum of 140 characters.

● This number tells you how many characters you have left in your message, if you need them.

④ Click **update**.

How can I post a tweet using my mobile phone?
The short format of Twitter messages is perfectly suited to text message capabilities of many mobile phones. For this reason, Twitter enables you to configure your mobile phone to send tweets. Click **Settings** and then click **Devices**. In the Mobile Phone section, type your mobile phone number and then click **Save**. To verify your number, send the code that Twitter displays to the specified number.

continued

Microblog with Twitter *(continued)*

You will mostly use Twitter to send tweets. However, Twitter is also a community that has millions of users, some of whom will be friends, family, colleagues, or simply people you find interesting. If you want to see the tweets that another Twitter user posts, you must *follow* that person.

Twitter is also useful as a conversation tool. If a person you are following posts a tweet that you find interesting or useful, you can send that person a reply to that tweet.

FOLLOW A TWITTER USER

① If you know that person's Twitter user name, go to twitter.com/*user* (where *user* is the person's user name).

② Click **Follow**.

● You can also click **Find People** and use the form to locate the person you want.

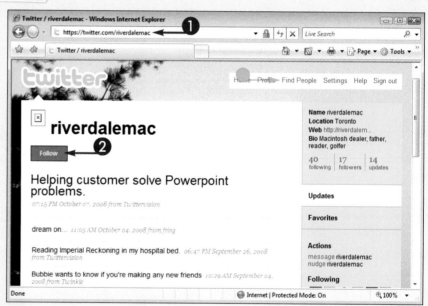

FOLLOW ONE OF YOUR FOLLOWERS

① If the person is already following you, click **Home**.

② Click **followers**.

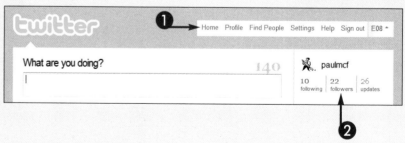

3 Click **follow** below the person's name.

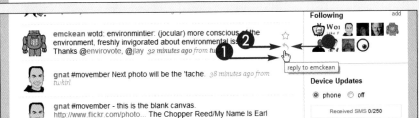

REPLY TO A TWEET

1 Position the mouse ⌖ over the post.

● Twitter displays an arrow icon (⬑).

2 Click that icon.

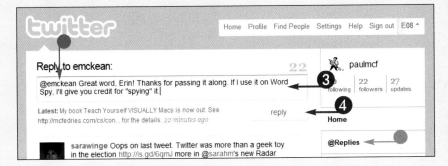

● Twitter adds @*User* to the post text box, where *User* is the user name of the person who sent the tweet.

3 Type your reply.

4 Click **reply**.

● To see the replies sent to you, click **Home** and then click **@Replies**.

How can I configure my Twitter account?

Twitter offers a number of configuration options that control things like your name, password, and picture. In your Twitter page, click **Settings** and then use the tabs to see the various options. For example, use the **Account** tab to change your name and e-mail address, and to specify a one-line bio. Use the **Password** tab to set your account password; use the **Devices** tab to configure mobile posts; and use the **Notices** tab to configure the notices that Twitter sends you.

Discover Other Blog Hosts

Although Blogger, TypePad, and WordPress, described earlier in this chapter, are the most popular blog hosting services, they are not the only blog hosts available to you. The Web is actually home to dozens of sites that can host your blog. However, most of these sites are too small, are poorly designed, offer few useful features, or are targeted at very specific types of bloggers.

In this section, you learn some basic information about seven popular and well-designed blog hosts suitable to most new bloggers, including Windows Live Spaces, LiveJournal, and Xanga.

Windows Live Spaces

Windows Live Spaces (spaces.live.com) is Microsoft's blog hosting service that offers an easy way to create, customize, and update a blog. You can also share photos and create lists of items such as books, music, and movies. You can post via e-mail, create an RSS feed, control comments, and even tie your Amazon Associates ID to your lists to earn affiliate income if people purchase things from your lists.

LiveJournal

LiveJournal (www.livejournal.com) was one of the most popular of the original blog hosts, and about 17 million people have used the service to create blogs (or *journals* as the site calls them). The service is free (although there are also paid accounts that offer more features), and each blog is part of a larger community of related blogs. You can even start your own community. The blogs have all the standard features, and you can post via e-mail, text message, or instant message.

Xanga

Xanga (www.xanga.com) is a blog service that offers both free and paid hosting. The free hosting service offers easy post creation, a decent rich text editor that supports colors, fonts, and other formatting options, and *skins* that enable you to control the look and layout of your blog.

The paid hosting service is called Xanga Premium, and for $4 per month ($25 per year) you get 10GB of image storage, more customization options, and the Xanga ads are removed from your pages.

BlogHarbor

BlogHarbor (www.blogharbor.com) is a full-featured blog host that offers two plans: the Standard plan gives 2GB of storage and 5GB of monthly bandwidth; the Plus plan gives 10GB of storage and 40GB of monthly bandwidth. Both plans offer category support, photo albums, online poll and survey creation, and RSS feeds. You can post via e-mail or mobile phone, and you can set up multiple authors.

BlogHarbor offers the easiest and most powerful wa
to-use templates and advanced weblogging features
BlogHarbor weblogs the best web publishing solution

Blog-City

Blog-City (www.blog-city.com) enables you to set up hosting for either a personal blog ($4.50 per month) or a collection of business blogs (starting at $99.88 per month). Personal blogs get 100MB of storage, 2GB of monthly bandwidth, and a maximum of 2,000 posts. You can post via e-mail and you can set up multiple authors.

Thoughts.com

Thoughts.com (www.thoughts.com) is a free host that offers very basic blogging features. Thoughts.com is only for personal blogs; you cannot use it to promote a business or to run an affiliate program. Thoughts.com also offers photo and video sharing, podcast distribution, and you can create your own online polls and surveys.

Squarespace

Squarespace (www.squarespace.com) is a premium blog hosting service that offers advanced online software for building, customizing, and adding content to your site. Depending on the plan you choose (rates run as low as $8 per month), you can not only create a sophisticated blog, but also add automated forms, photo galleries, forums, and lots more. A 14-day free trial is available.

Get the Most Out of Your Blog

Getting the most out of your blog means two things. First, it means creating posts and other content that you are proud of and that you want to share with the world.

Second, it means building an audience. Just because you have created your own blog, it does not mean that it will automatically be a success. That may not matter much if you are blogging only for a select group of family, friends, or colleagues. However, it is more likely that you want a wider audience, and there are a few techniques you can use to attract and keep visitors.

Post Regularly

A blog is, by definition, a site that gets regular updates. If people know that a blog offers fresh content regularly, they will be more likely to revisit and to recommend the blog to others. If you only post every few weeks, you will be unlikely to attract or hold an audience. If you cannot post for a while for some reason, let people know that your site will be quiet temporarily.

Choose Your Theme Wisely

To help you post regularly, choose a good blog theme up front. The topic should be something that fascinates you, but do not make the common beginning blogger mistake of tackling a topic that's too big for one person to handle (such as "Technology" or "The Arts"). You need to narrow things down to a subset or two that particularly interests you and that will still generate enough content to keep your blog alive (such as "Building Computers" or "Espionage Books").

Create a Catchy Name

With millions of blogs now online, standing out in the crowd is difficult. You can help yourself in that department by coming up with a good name for your blog. In general, a shorter name is better than an overly long one because it will be easier for people to remember. A name that uses an apt pun is a good way to go because it shows off your wit and helps the name stand out. Finally, as far as possible (particularly considering my injunction to keep the name short), your name should in some way reflect the overall topic or theme of your blog.

Provide Nonstandard Links

You will not gain any new readers or keep your existing readers if all your links are to obvious mainstream media stories. Either try to locate the obscure mainstream media stories buried deep inside their Web sites or, even better, try to find links to interesting things in the more obscure sites: the alternative press, e-zines, personal pages, and so on. Developing a reputation as someone who regularly finds interesting stories from the Web's less traveled locales will drive a lot of people to your blog.

Write Short Posts

Throughout their short history, blogs have been characterized by short entries, and to this day most blogs consist of short, easily digested entries. More important, blog readers expect entries to be short. In other words, if a blogger consistently posts long-winded entries, his readers will often either complain or go elsewhere. Therefore, make sure that most of your posts are relatively short. If an entry seems too long, cut out any unnecessary words or sentences. Look for redundant words or multiple sentences that essentially say the same thing.

Stay Relevant

A good way to keep your posts short is to stick to your blog's main theme, or themes. Few things are as frustrating for a reader as an undisciplined blog writer who constantly goes off on tangents and digressions about whatever comes into his or her head. Stay on topic and your readers will stay with you.

Get On the Search Engines

To help others find your blog, be sure to submit your site to the major search engines, including Google (www.google.com/intl/en_ extra/addurl.html), MSN Live Search (search. msn.com/docs/submit.aspx), and Yahoo! (search.yahoo.com/info/submit.html). You should also sign up for an account on Technorati (www.technorati.com), the blog search engine, and claim your blog.

Join a Blogring

A *webring* is a collection of related Web sites that uses special links to create a kind of chain that connects one site to another. This enables users to easily surf through a group of sites that are all focused on a particular topic. If all the sites are blogs, it is called a *blogring* and joining one is a great way to get traffic to your blog. Use your favorite search engine to search for **topic blogring**, where *topic* is a word or phrase that describes the topic of your blog. You can also try RingSurf (www.ringsurf. com), a directory of webrings.

Comment on a Blog Post

Most blogs are improved by the addition of intelligent and knowledgeable comments. If you want to participate in the conversation that ensues after a blog post, you need to know how to add a comment.

One of the great appeals of a blog is not only the quality posts that it publishes, but the comments that often accompany such posts. Although comments are often trivial or imprudent, many offer smart and useful feedback on the post, as well as knowledgeable and savvy information beyond the post. By adding quality comments yourself, you add to the overall quality of a blog.

Comment on a Blog Post

① Navigate to the post you want to comment on.

② Click the **Comments** link.

● The site displays the existing comments, if any.

③ If the site requires an account to post comments, click the **Sign in** link.

Note: If the current blog does not require an account to post comments, skip to step 7.

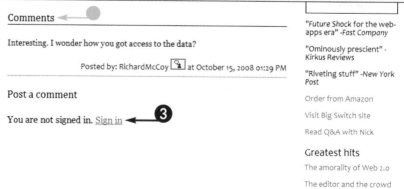

The sign in form appears.

Note: *This procedure varies from site to site.*

④ Type your user name.

⑤ Type your password.

⑥ Click **Sign In**.

The comment form appears.

⑦ Type your comment.

⑧ Click **Post**.

The site posts your comment.

Why does my comment not appear on the site right away?

Many sites experience comment problems such as people who submit only abusive or profane comments, or unscrupulous advertisers who post only spam messages as comments. To thwart these users, many bloggers *moderate* their comments. This means that each comment is checked by the blogger when it is submitted. If the blogger judges the comment to be appropriate, he or she allows the comment to be posted. This usually takes a bit of time, so your comment may not appear for a while.

Are there etiquette guidelines to follow when commenting on blog posts?

When commenting on an entry, keep your text confined to the substance of that entry. Do not write about something totally unrelated just because you know it will be posted for others to read. If another commenter writes something that you find rude or insulting, do not respond in kind. Instead, either ignore the offender or try to respond with a well-articulated argument. Never use a comment to advertise a product or service. If you are a blogger, include a link to your blog in your comment.

Subscribe to a Blog Feed

You can keep up to date with a blog's posts by subscribing to its feed, which displays the latest site content.

Keeping up with your favorite blogs is often time consuming. To solve this problem, many blogs maintain feeds, which are also called RSS feeds (RSS stands for Really Simple Syndication).

A *feed* is a special file that contains the most recent information added to the site. You can use Internet Explorer or Safari to subscribe to a site's Web feed. This makes it easy to view the feed any time you want to see the site's new content.

Subscribe to a Blog Feed

SUBSCRIBE TO A BLOG FEED USING INTERNET EXPLORER

1 Navigate to the blog that provides the feed.

2 Click the feed icon (🔊).

● If the site has multiple feeds, click ⊡ and then click the feed you want.

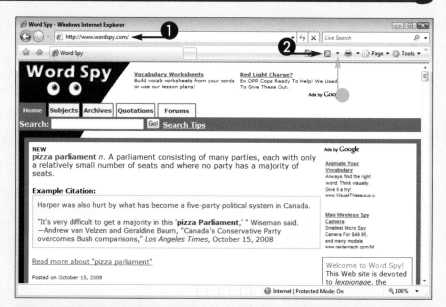

Internet Explorer displays the feed.

3 Click **Subscribe to this feed**.

The Subscribe to this Feed dialog box appears.

4 Click **Subscribe**.

Internet Explorer adds a subscription to the feed.

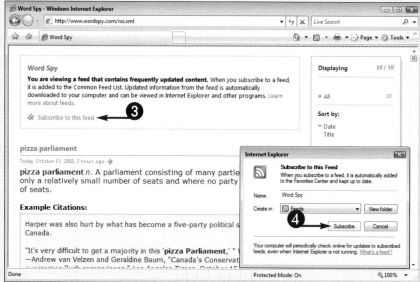

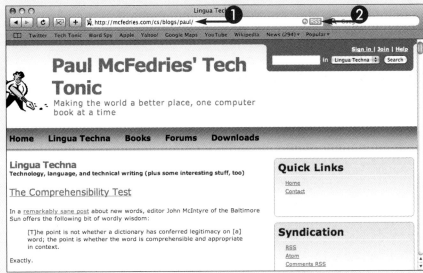

SUBSCRIBE TO A BLOG FEED USING SAFARI

1 Navigate to the blog that provides the feed.

2 Click **RSS**.

Note: *If the site has multiple feeds, a list of those feeds appears, so click the feed you want.*

Safari displays the feed.

3 Click **Subscribe in Mail**.

Your Mac opens the Mail application and adds the feed to the RSS section.

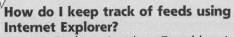

How do I keep track of feeds using Internet Explorer?
Internet Explorer (versions 7 and later) maintains a Feeds list that contains all of the feeds you are subscribed to. To see this list, click the **Favorites Center** icon (⭐) or press **Alt** + **C**, then click the **Feeds** button. If a feed title appears in bold type, it means the feed has new posts since the last time you viewed it. To view a feed, click it in the Feeds list.

Are there other methods I can use to subscribe to feeds?
Yes, there are separate programs and services called *feed readers* (sometimes called *RSS readers*) that you can use. For example, the latest versions of Microsoft Outlook come with a feed reader built in, and you can also download Newz Crawler (www.newzcrawler. com). Online feed readers include Google Reader (www.google.com/reader), Newsgator (www. newsgator.com), FeedDemon (www.feeddemon. com), and Bloglines (www.bloglines.com).

Index

Index

Index

length, password, 74
libraries, 98
Library of Congress, 98
Line jack, 16
Lineage II game, 103
LinkedIn, 138–139
links, 6, 34–35, 44, 238
list owner, 180
live media stream, 124
Live Search Farecast, 106
live streaming, 124
LiveJournal, 236
local area network (LAN), 4
lock icon, Web browser, 59, 193
Lonely Planet, 107
Lord of the Rings Online, 103
lurking, 182

M

Mac instant messaging, 204–205
Mac OS X, 29. **See also** Mac OS X Mail
Mac OS X Firewall, 31
Mac OS X Mail
    attachments, 169, 173
    Display remote images in HTML messages option, 188
    forwarding, 177
    receiving mail, 171
    replying, 175
    sending, 167
Macromedia HomeSite, 112
magazines, 96
mail, 64. **See** also e-mail
mailing lists, 180–183
Make Friends Online site, 100
mandatory fields, Web form, 47
mapping services, 107
MapQuest, 107
MarketWatch, 105
massively multiplayer online game (MMOG), 103
massively multiplayer online role playing game (MMORPG), 103
McAfee Internet Security Suite, 68, 191
media
    Google Maps, 128–129
    music, 116–117
    overview, 7
    photo sharing, 122–123
    playing, 11
    podcast, subscribing to, 118–119
    radio, 120–121
    streaming, 124–125
    YouTube videos, 126–127
Media Player, 120–121, 124
Medium security level, 63
meebo Web IM, 201

Meetup site, 143
Merrill Lynch Direct, 105
message boards, 101
message previews, e-mail, 163
microblogging, 232–235
Microsoft Password Checker, 74
Miniclip site, 102
MMOG (massively multiplayer online game), 103
MMORPG (massively multiplayer online role playing game), 103
mobile phone posts, Twitter, 233
mobile updates, 133
MobileMe accounts, iChat, 205
modems, 5, 16–17
moderator, mailing list, 180
Monster job board, 109
Motion Picture Experts Group Audio Level 3 (MP3), 116
The Motley Fool site, 105
movie sites, streaming, 125
MovieFlix site, 125
Movielink site, 125
MP3 (Motion Picture Experts Group Audio Level 3), 116
MSN Bill Pay, 104
MSN Games, 102
MSN Groups, 101
MSN Live Search, 239
MSN Money, 105
MSN Web Messenger, 201
MSNBC, 96, 125
MTV, 125
multiple e-mail addresses, 165
multi-user domain (MUD) games, 103
Museum Stuff site, 98
museums, 98
music, 116–117
MyCheckFree site, 104
MySpace, 136–137

N

names, blog, 238
Napster, 117
nature-related sites, 111
Net Nanny, 61
Netflix, 125
netiquette, 144, 178
network card port, 17
networking. **See** social networking
New York Public Library, 98
news, 10, 96–97
news feed, 10
news portals, 97
news syndication, 97
Newsgator, 97, 243
newsgroup addresses, 189

Index

Index

Index

Read Less–Learn More®

Visual®

There's a Visual book for every learning level...

Simplified®

The place to start if you're new to computers. Full color.

- Computers
- Creating Web Pages
- Mac OS
- Office
- Windows

Teach Yourself VISUALLY™

Get beginning to intermediate-level training in a variety of topics. Full color.

- Access
- Bridge
- Chess
- Computers
- Crocheting
- Digital Photography
- Dog training
- Dreamweaver
- Excel
- Flash
- Golf
- Guitar
- Handspinning
- HTML
- Jewelry Making & Beading
- Knitting
- Mac OS
- Office
- Photoshop
- Photoshop Elements
- Piano
- Poker
- PowerPoint
- Quilting
- Scrapbooking
- Sewing
- Windows
- Wireless Networking
- Word

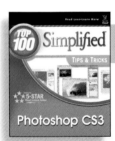

Top 100 Simplified® Tips & Tricks

Tips and techniques to take your skills beyond the basics. Full color.

- Digital Photography
- eBay
- Excel
- Google
- Internet
- Mac OS
- Office
- Photoshop
- Photoshop Elements
- PowerPoint
- Windows

...all designed for visual learners—just like you!

Master VISUALLY®

Your complete visual reference. Two-color interior.

- 3ds Max
- Creating Web Pages
- Dreamweaver and Flash
- Excel
- Excel VBA Programming

- iPod and iTunes
- Mac OS
- Office
- Optimizing PC Performance
- Photoshop Elements

- QuickBooks
- Quicken
- Windows
- Windows Mobile
- Windows Server

Visual Blueprint™

Where to go for professional-level programming instruction. Two-color interior.

- Ajax
- ASP.NET 2.0
- Excel Data Analysis
- Excel Pivot Tables
- Excel Programming

- HTML
- JavaScript
- Mambo
- PHP & MySQL
- SEO

- Vista Sidebar
- Visual Basic
- XML

Visual Encyclopedia™

Your A to Z reference of tools and techniques. Full color.

- Dreamweaver
- Excel
- Mac OS

- Photoshop
- Windows

Visual Quick Tips

Shortcuts, tricks, and techniques for getting more done in less time. Full color.

- Crochet
- Digital Photography
- Excel
- iPod & iTunes

- Knitting
- MySpace
- Office
- PowerPoint

- Windows
- Wireless Networking

For a complete listing of Visual books, go to wiley.com/go/visual

Visual®
An Imprint of ⊕WILEY
Now you know.